1001

Ways to

Calm

1001

Ways to

Calm

ARCTURUS

With special thanks to Paul Lucas

ARCTURUS

This edition published in 2025 by Arcturus Publishing Limited
26/27 Bickels Yard, 151–153 Bermondsey Street,
London SE1 3HA

ISBN: 978- 1-3988-6028-5
AD012873NT

Printed in China

Contents

Introduction

As our lives become increasingly hectic it's ever more important that we find refuges of calm and relaxation. Yet often the more we seek calmness the harder it seems to find. The very act of searching can leave us even more frustrated and anxious than when we started.

This little book is designed to act as a guide to steer you towards your own garden of calm, whenever you need to find it. It will reassure you that tranquillity can be found in the most unlikely places, and remind you that it is not where you look but how you see that determines whether you find your haven of peace. A mixture of inspirational quotes, ideas and practical tips that will help you to relax and maintain your equilibrium, whether you're on your own or with others, at home or at work. Dip into the pages that follow whenever life threatens to overwhelm you, and allow the calming voices within to transport you to the sanctuary of calm that you carry within you at all times, no matter how far away this may sometimes appear to be.

What is Calm?

How do we define calm?
How can we ever hope
to find it unless we know
what we are looking for?

In great moments life seems neither right nor wrong, but something greater: it seems inevitable.
Margaret Sherwood

Tranquillity can be found in the tiniest of moments, like when you take a single deep breath in the middle of a busy day.

Just doing one thing at a time is a good principle to follow.

Often just being around familiar things can make you feel calm.

Slow down and you might find that the dreams you thought you were chasing were actually trying to catch up with you.

Serenity is knowing that your worst shot is still pretty good.

Johnny Miller

Making things easier for yourself should never make you feel guilty.

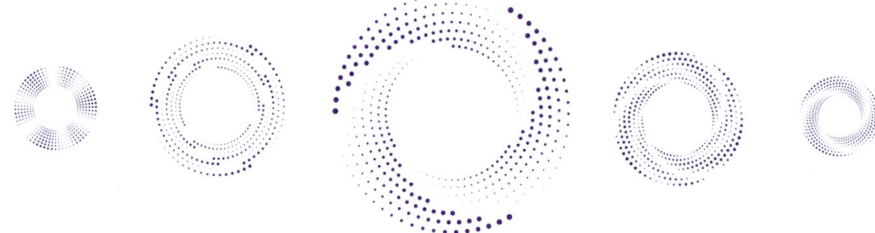

Tranquillity is being able to relax when you don't have time to.

The ideal of calm
exists in a sitting cat.
Jules Renard

Nature does not fear change and neither should you. Each new season is beautiful in its own way.

The first step to tranquillity is acceptance.

Boredom is the feeling that everything is a waste of time; serenity, that *nothing* is.
Thomas Szasz

If you feel you are part of the world rather than separate from it, then you are becoming tranquil.

You will never find true tranquillity until you learn to love yourself.

Be positive and you will attract positive things.

It's not so much how busy you are, but why you are busy. The bee is praised; the mosquito is swatted.
Marie O'Connor

When you find your inner equilibrium, work becomes almost effortless.

Focus on your needs rather than your desires in order to find tranquillity.

Don't try and 'fit in'. Just try and be who you really are.

All of the animals, excepting man, know that the principal business of life is to enjoy it.
Samuel Butler

Tranquillity is an attitude rather than a destination.

Knowing that
nothing lasts forever
can produce a
wonderful sense
of calm.

Anxiety is caused by thinking you should be someone else. Tranquillity comes when you relax and enjoy being yourself.

Don't believe you are too busy to indulge yourself; even the briefest moments of relaxation can invigorate you for the rest of the day.

What is life but the angle of vision? A man is measured by the angle at which he looks at objects.
Ralph Waldo Emerson

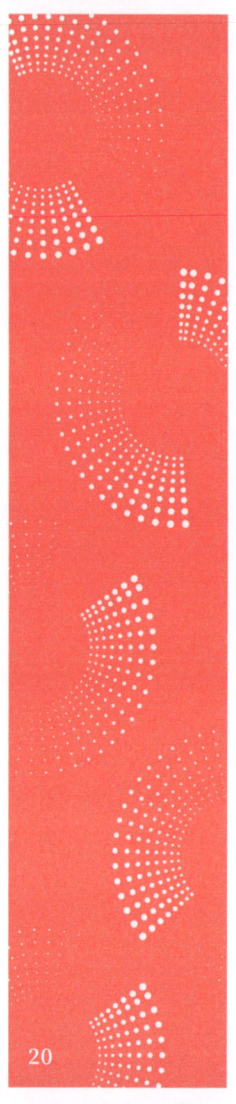

You will find tranquillity when you truly feel you deserve it.

Impatience is the enemy of tranquillity.

Imagine a tranquil setting
and you will immediately
reduce your level of anxiety.

**How blessed are some people, whose
lives have no fears, no dreads, to whom
sleep is a blessing that comes nightly,
and brings nothing but sweet dreams.**
Bram Stoker

Write down pleasant dreams
so that you can revisit them
when you are under stress.

It is often hard to feel truly tranquil when surrounded by material things.

Calm self-confidence is as far from conceit as the desire to earn a decent living is remote from greed.

Channing Pollock

If you don't open
the doors of your
mind now and then,
stress will never be
able to leave you.

If only we'd stop trying to be happy we'd have a pretty good time.
Edith Wharton

Don't overlook the miraculous nature of seemingly ordinary things.

If you don't give yourself permission to be tranquil, how will you ever find peace?

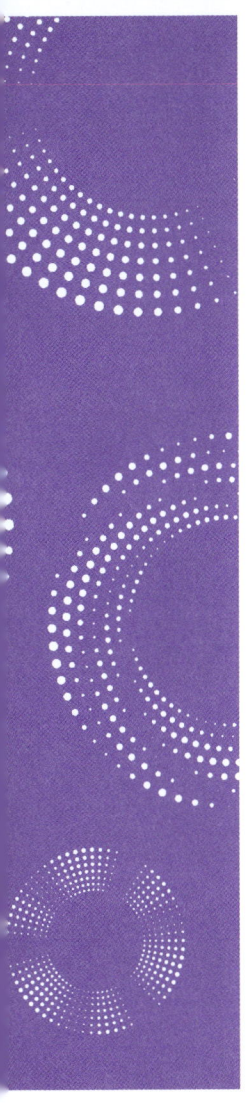

When they are alone they want to be with others, and when they are with others they want to be alone. After all, human beings are like that.

Gertrude Stein

There are neither yesterdays nor tomorrows, there is only here and now.

Remind yourself that to keep going is a type of victory.

There is no pleasure in having nothing to do; the fun is in having lots to do and not doing it.
Mary Wilson Little

Don't imagine that everyone else is more contented than you are.

Thinking positive is the first major step on the path to tranquillity.

Millions long for immortality who don't know what to do with themselves on a rainy afternoon.
Susan Ertz

Take time off when you feel under the weather. Continuing to work will only make it worse.

Be happy whenever you have done your best, no matter what the result.

Not taking risks can be as stressful as taking risks.

29

> Don't sweat the small stuff...
> and it is all small stuff.
>
> *Richard Carlson*

When you are unhappy, is there anything more maddening than to be told that you should be contented with your lot?

Kathleen Norris

Accepting
that life is full
of pressures is
a key step to
finding calm.

Sometimes you have to bite your tongue and just let things go.

Don't be afraid to dream big.

Seeing things from other people's perspective helps to bring harmony into your life.

Better by far you should forget
and smile than that you should
remember and be sad.
Christina Rossetti

**Don't be afraid to ask
others for help.**

**Be curious: understanding
leads, ultimately, to tranquillity.**

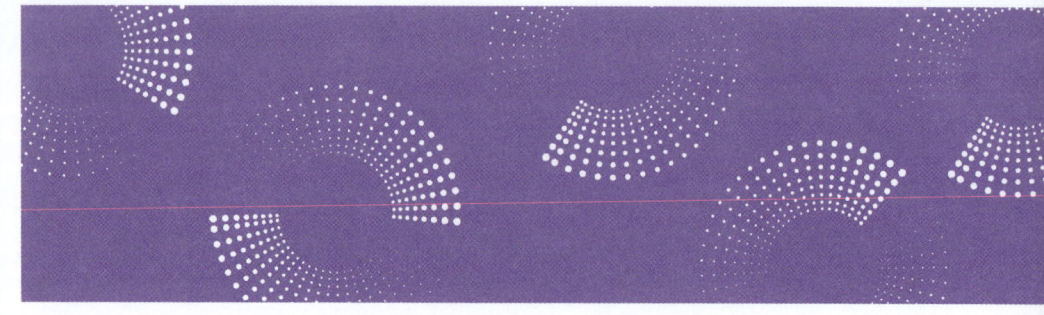

To achieve the impossible dream, try going to sleep.
Joan Klempner

You will never find calm by ignoring reality.

It doesn't matter what you believe as long as your life has meaning. If it doesn't, you will always feel anxious.

If you realize too acutely how valuable time is, you are too paralyzed to do anything.

Katharine Butler Hathaway

Serenity is something you choose, not something that happens to you.

I don't own an inch of land, but all I see is mine.
Lucy Larcom

Swim with the tide rather than against it whenever possible.

Fear cannot be banished, but it can be calm and without panic; it can be mitigated by reason and evaluation.

Vannevar Bush

Make friends with your inner child and you'll never be far from calm.

Let go of your anger or it will always poison your heart.

Confront your fears: they are what prevent you from finding tranquillity.

The secret to finding tranquillity lies in self-control.

A hot bath can help in
so many situations.
Self-soothe with lovely
bath salts and a long soak.

We can never hope to
understand anything
completely: remind
yourself that not
knowing is okay.

Remind yourself of what really matters to you, and pursue only that. If you follow your heart, then you will find inner peace along the way.

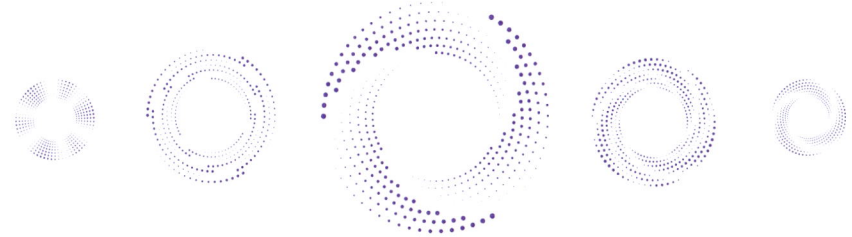

There are two ways of meeting difficulties. You alter the difficulties or you alter yourself to meet them.

Phyllis Bottome

I still miss those I loved who are no longer with me but I find I am grateful for having loved them. The gratitude has finally conquered the loss.
Rita Mae Brown

Selfishness is perhaps the biggest barrier to tranquillity.

Half our life is spent trying to find something to do with the time we have rushed through life trying to save.
Will Rogers

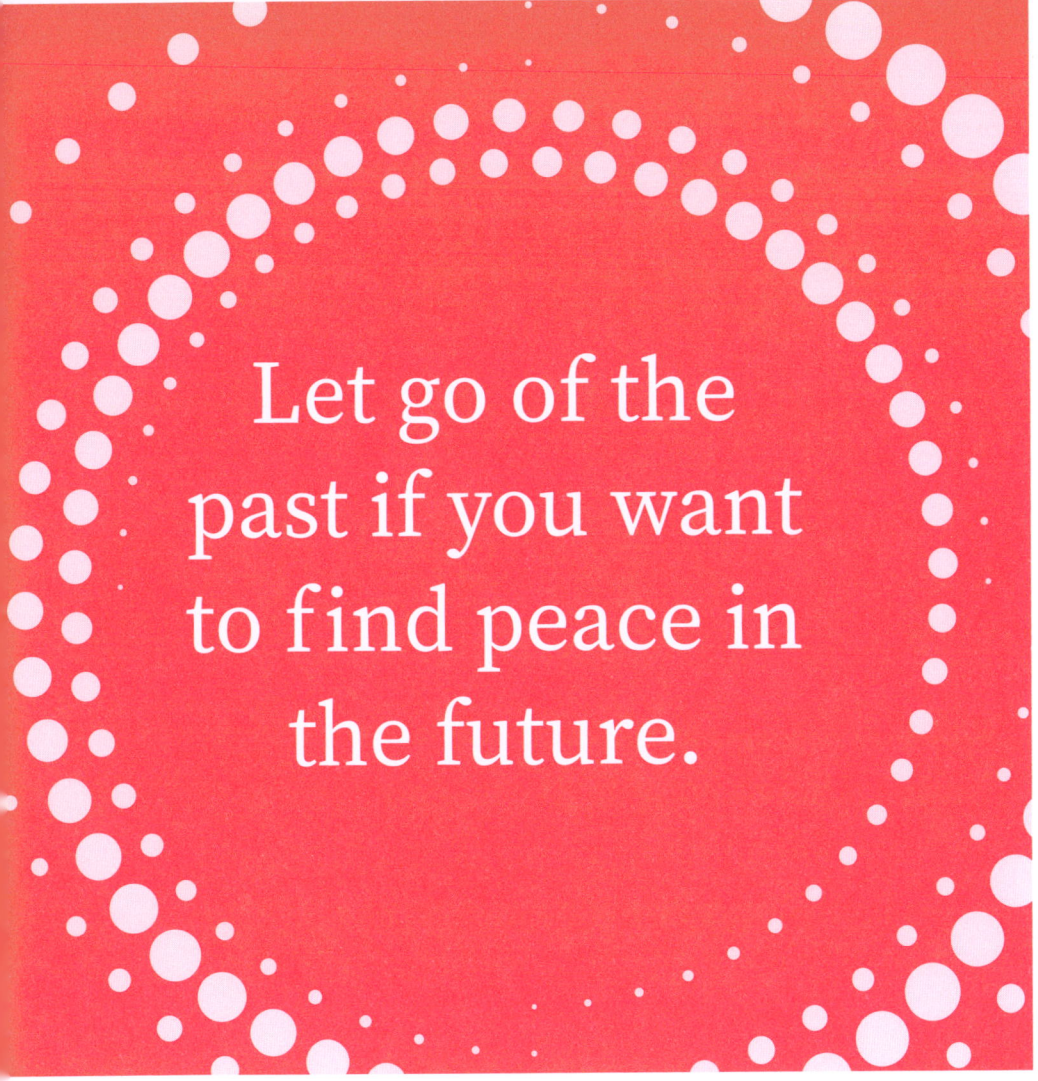

Let go of the past if you want to find peace in the future.

To find true tranquillity you need to be at peace not just with yourself but also with others, so strive to find the good in everyone you meet.

Weather means more when you have a garden. There's nothing like listening to a shower and thinking how it is soaking in around your green beans.
Marcelene Cox

Remind yourself that you are important, special and unique.

Leave the phone to ring now and then: you'll soon realize that if the call is important then the caller will phone back.

Work, look for peace and calm in work: you will find it nowhere else.
Dmitri Mendeleev

If you focus on doing something well you will often find tranquillity creeps up on you without you even realizing it.

Make the most of what you have rather than worrying about what you don't have.

To hear pure silence you have to listen hard.

While conscience is our friend, all is at peace; however once it is offended, farewell to a tranquil mind.

Lady Mary Wortley Montagu

To find peace, give love.

Tranquillity is whatever makes you feel most like yourself.

There is more to life than increasing its speed.
Mahatma Gandhi

Calm tends to descend upon those who remember to laugh at themselves.

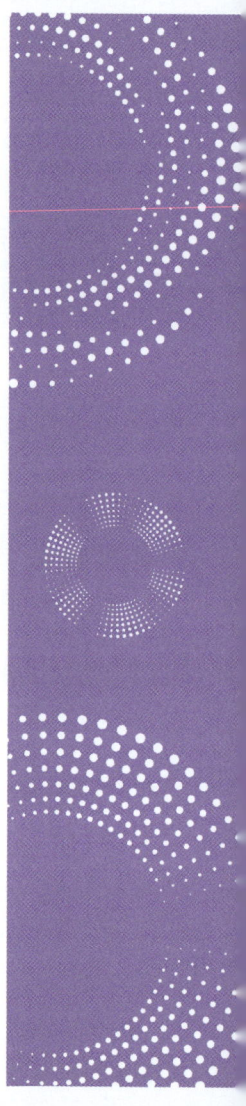

If you carry tranquillity in your heart you can be at peace even amongst a bustling crowd.

You can't be everything to everybody, so concentrate on just being everything you can be to yourself.

True silence is the rest of the mind; it is to the spirit what sleep is to the body, nourishment and refreshment.
William Penn

Don't compare yourself to other people; just be content to be yourself.

Try and look at everything as if you were viewing it for the first time.

Sometimes just slowing down slightly is as relaxing as a rest.

Tranquillity arrives in its own good time: don't try and hurry it along.

Gratitude changes the pangs of memory into a tranquil joy.
Dietrich Bonhoeffer

Don't overthink things, or you will never be at peace.

Take a detour from the main road now and then: tranquillity lurks in the strangest nooks and crannies.

It is impossible to enjoy idling thoroughly unless one has plenty of work to do.

Jerome K. Jerome

Trusting
in others will
bring you peace.

The greatest weapon against stress is our ability to choose one thought over another.

William James

If your expectations of yourself
are too high, then you will always
be disappointed in yourself.

The more
you learn to like
yourself the more
you will enjoy
spending time
with yourself.

Take responsibility for your choices and you'll start to feel more in control of your life.

There is no need to go to India or anywhere else to find peace. You will find that deep place of silence right in your room, your garden or even your bathtub.

Elisabeth Kübler-Ross

Do not worry unduly about financial matters. There is more to life than money.

Happiness is the harvest of a quiet eye.

Austin O'Malley

Stress is an ignorant state. It believes that everything is an emergency.

Natalie Goldberg

Learn to only concern yourself with things you can actually change.

All the tranquillity you crave is already within you; you just need to find ways to access it.

Don't be afraid of what others think of you. All that matters is what you think of yourself.

> **To sit with a dog on a hillside on a glorious afternoon is to be back in Eden, where doing nothing was not boring – it was peace.**
>
> *Milan Kundera*

Examine your strengths and weaknesses calmly, for tranquillity is impossible without honesty.

Finding Calm

Are calm places rare and far away, or are they all around us? Some people seem to walk through life in a cloud of calm, so why does calm seem so elusive to so many of us?

Have courage and learn to be patient, and you will find tranquillity in everything you do.

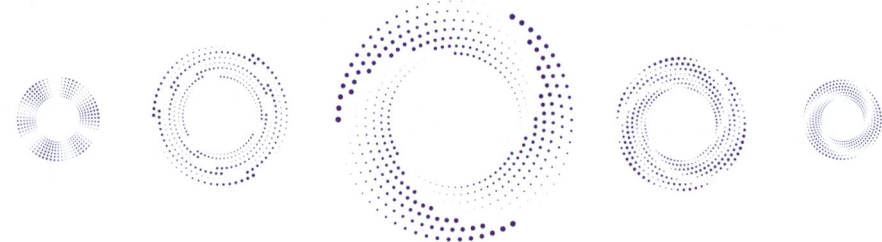

Attune yourself to the pace of nature, as the natural world has infinite patience.

Sometimes to find a calm place you must first walk through a storm.

People travel to wonder at the height of mountains, at the huge waves of the sea, at the long courses of rivers, at the vast compass of the ocean, at the circular motion of the stars; and they pass by themselves without wondering.
St Augustine

It is hard to remain calm when you are suffering, but tranquillity often helps to heal your wounds.

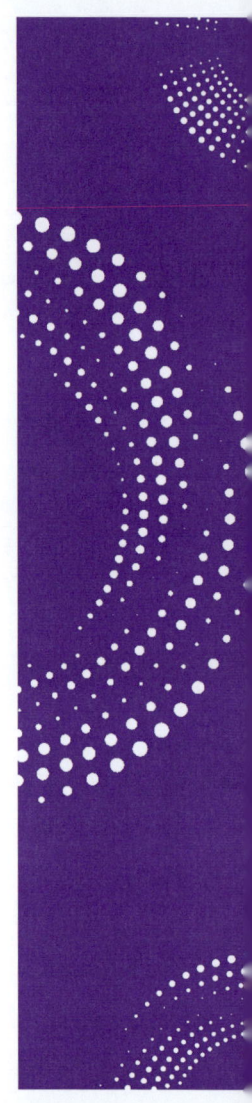

Forget the past and live the present hour.

Sarah Knowles Bolton

Hard work often goes to waste when it is not the product of a tranquil mind.

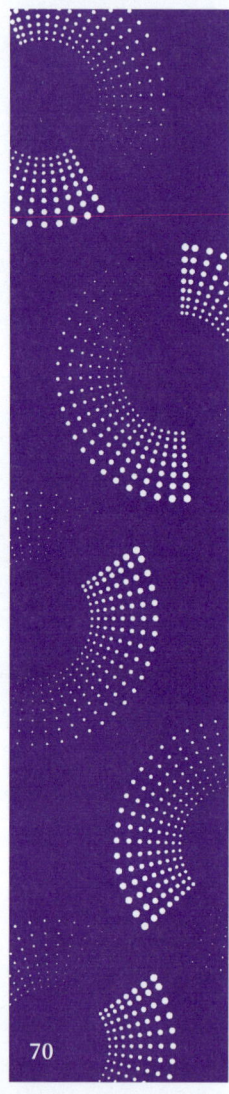

You do not need to leave your room. Remain sitting at your table and listen. Do not even listen, simply wait, be quiet, still and solitary. The world will freely offer itself to you to be unmasked, it has no choice, it will roll in ecstasy at your feet.

Franz Kafka

Place lavender under your pillow for a good night's rest.

Look up and not down;
look forward and not back; look
out and not in; and lend a hand.

E. E. Hale

Problems tend to shrink in size
when viewed with a calm eye.

True tranquillity is a combination of acceptance and hope.

I shut my eyes in order to see.
Paul Gauguin

Those who are tranquil live longer than those who strive.

Often the quickest way to find tranquillity is to turn away from stressful situations.

Force yourself to laugh now and then, and you will often realize that things are not nearly as bad as they seem.

Let your mind wander, and try and block any conscious thoughts that come into your head.

Concentrate on one of your five senses and allow a smell, touch, taste, sight or sound to fill your world for a moment.

Running is a great way to relieve stress and clear the mind.
Joan Van Ark

Make sure staying calm is always at the top of your list of options.

Close your eyes and allow your entire body to relax, from your temples down to your toes. A fully relaxed body in turn leads to a relaxed mind.

Eat healthily and you'll feel better for it. In particular eat more alkaline foods than acidic foods.

Take rest; a field that has rested gives a bountiful crop. *Ovid*

Get off the bus or train one stop early and treat yourself to a short walk.

No one can get inner peace by pouncing on it. *Harry Emerson Fosdick*

Treat problems as if they were ripples on the surface of the ocean, and imagine yourself being as still and calm as the waters on the sea bed.

Tranquillity never finds those who are running away from themselves.

Don't confuse tranquillity with taking the easy option. To be tranquil you must be true to yourself, which sometimes means making difficult decisions.

Keep a diary, and write down when you have felt stressed and when you have felt calm. Try and find patterns and then avoid the situations that threaten your tranquillity.

If you follow your bliss, you put yourself on a kind of track that has been there all the while, waiting for you, and the life that you ought to be living is the one you are living. When you can see that, you begin to meet people who are in your field of bliss, and they open doors to you. I say, follow your bliss and don't be afraid, and doors will open where you didn't know they were going to be.

Joseph Campbell

Good humor is a tonic for mind and body. It is the best antidote for anxiety and depression. It is a business asset. It attracts and keeps friends. It lightens human burdens. It is the direct route to serenity and contentment.

Grenville Kleiser

Stop. Take a deep breath. Do this at least once every hour to maintain your tranquillity throughout the day.

Sit in a church for half an hour. It doesn't matter if you are not religious – sacred spaces are always peaceful places.

When you feel you know nothing, don't become frustrated but instead celebrate the mystery of life.

A happy life must be to a great extent a quiet life, for it is only in an atmosphere of quiet that true joy dare live.

Bertrand Russell

Arranging a bowl of flowers in the morning can give a sense of quiet in a crowded day – like writing a poem or saying a prayer.
Anne Morrow Lindbergh

Play is as important to adults as it is to children.

Sometimes I get up very early in the morning and enjoy a quiet house and cup of tea before the craziness begins. Other times, I'll take a quick walk on the beach. You can find peace in a few minutes.
Cindy Crawford

A positive outlook can turn envy into awe and frustration into patience.

Sing to yourself, even if you're too shy to sing out loud. Songs lift the spirit and calm the heart.

Every now and then just go somewhere else. It doesn't have to be far from home – any change of scenery will help you to relax.

All miseries derive from not being able to sit in a quiet room alone.
Blaise Pascal

Write a list of the things that you associate with tranquillity and then try and include some of those things in your day-to-day routine.

Beauty is not in the face; beauty is a light in the heart.

Kahlil Gibran

In the attitude of silence
the soul finds the path in
a clearer light, and what
is elusive and deceptive
resolves itself into
crystal clearness.
Our life is a long and
arduous quest after Truth.

Mahatma Gandhi

Seek out the sea, a lake or even a small pond. Nothing relaxes us like water.

Take life a day at a time; problems seem more manageable that way.

Engage with the natural world. Watching fish swim, birds fly or even spiders spinning webs all help to relax the mind.

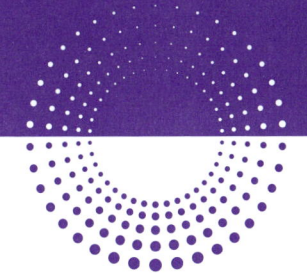

Surround yourself with calm people and you will soon discover that tranquillity is contagious.

Everybody should have personal sounds to listen for – sounds that will make [them feel] exhilarated and alive or quiet and calm... One of the greatest sounds of them all – and to me it is a sound – is utter, complete silence.

André Kostelanetz

It is never 'the wrong time' to take a break.

God never did make a more calm, quiet, innocent recreation than angling.

Izaak Walton

Listen out for untrue thoughts that can cause you stress.

Take time out to watch the sunset at least once a week.

Treat yourself to a massage.

Curiosity endows the people who have it with a generosity in argument and a serenity in their own mode of life which springs from heir cheerful willingness to let life take the form it will.

Alistair Cooke

Serenity
is a type of
freedom.

If your needs are few, finding tranquillity becomes a great deal easier.

Do nothing for at least an hour before you go to bed. You will find the time relaxing and you will sleep more soundly too.

Patience and fortitude are the twin pillars of inner peace.

The secret of success is to be in harmony with existence, to be always calm to let each wave of life wash us a little farther up the shore.

Cyril Connolly

Achieving tranquillity is often a matter of doing nothing.

If you value tranquillity, choose to remain quiet rather than speak ill of others.

Silence is more musical than any song.
Christina Rossetti

...I do know focusing on the exterior doesn't make me happy. If I want peace and serenity, it won't be reached by getting thinner or fatter.

Elle Macpherson

Those who complain are rarely tranquil.

Try growing something, even if it is only carrot tops in a saucer of water. Nurturing is a great way to relax.

All too often what stands between a person and tranquillity is their own fear.

Nothing gives you a sense of perspective like climbing mountains.

With the coming of spring, I am calm again.
Gustav Mahler

Be still, and allow tranquillity to gradually soak into you.

Only those who truly know themselves can ever be tranquil.

You must create tranquillity rather than searching for it.

Night, the beloved. Night, when words fade and things come alive. When the destructive analysis of day is done, and all that is truly important becomes whole and sound again. When man reassembles his fragmentary self and grows with the calm of a tree.

Antoine de Saint-Exupéry

Tranquillity cannot be separated from personal responsibility.

Relax your posture: if you are hunched and stiff you will feel tense on the inside as well as on the outside.

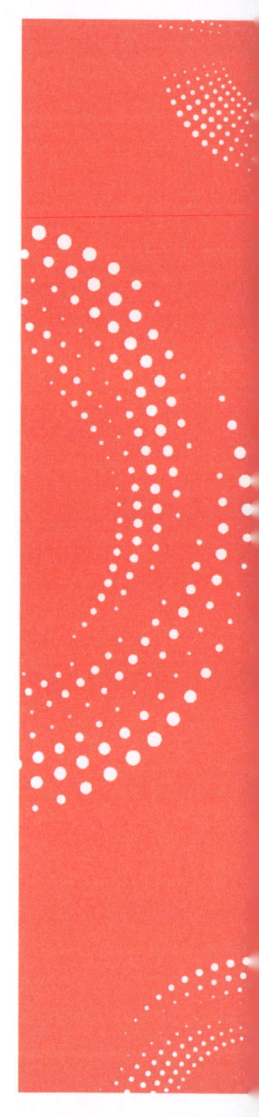

Silence is exhilarating at first
– as noise is –
but there is a sweetness
to silence outlasting
exhilaration, akin to the
sweetness of listening and
the velvet of sleep.
Edward Hoagland

Calmness is the art of feeling
at home wherever you may be.

Evolution changes the world more profoundly than revolution.

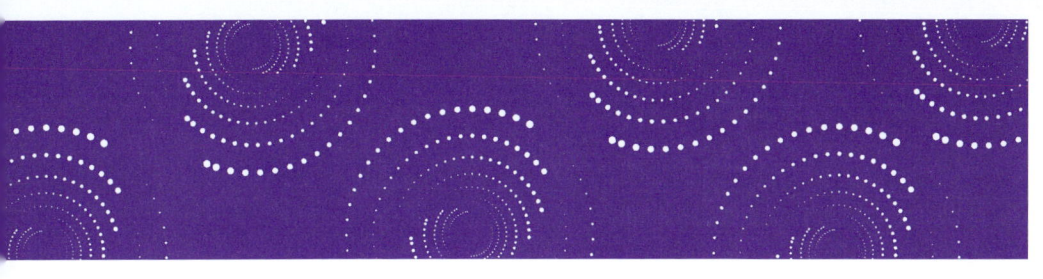

Try getting up an hour earlier than usual and savouring the quiet time before the rest of the world is awake.

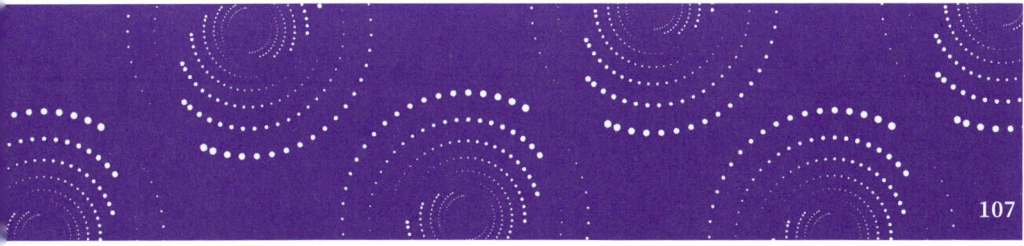

In every out-thrust headland, in every curving beach, in every grain of sand, there is the story of the earth.

Rachel Carson

Lie down in the dark for a few minutes and many of your problems will melt away.

Life goes by fast. Enjoy it. Calm down. It's all funny.

Joan Rivers

The language of tranquillity has to be learned in the same way as any other language has to be learned.

The final wisdom of life requires not the annulment of incongruity but the achievement of serenity within and above it.

Reinhold Niebuhr

The Arctic expresses the sum of all wisdom: Silence.
Walter Bauer

Soak a towel in hot water and place it around your neck to soothe you.

Take regular short sips of water throughout the day.

Concentrate on treading gently when you walk.

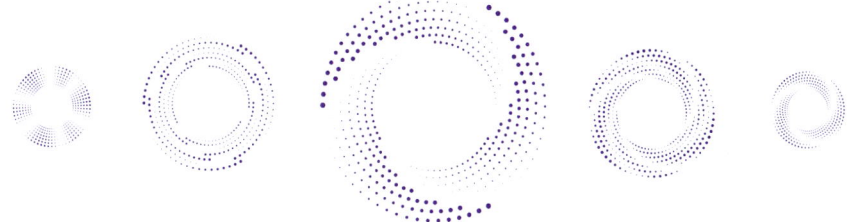

Keep your home and workplace tidy and you'll find they are more relaxing places to spend time in.

There are no barriers
to tranquillity that
cannot be overcome.

Every now and then,
put your phone down
and forget the time.

What is a television apparatus
to man, who has only to shut his
eyes to see the most inaccessible
regions of the seen and the never
seen, who has only to imagine
in order to pierce through walls
and cause all the planetary
Baghdads of his dreams to
rise from the dust.

Salvador Dalí

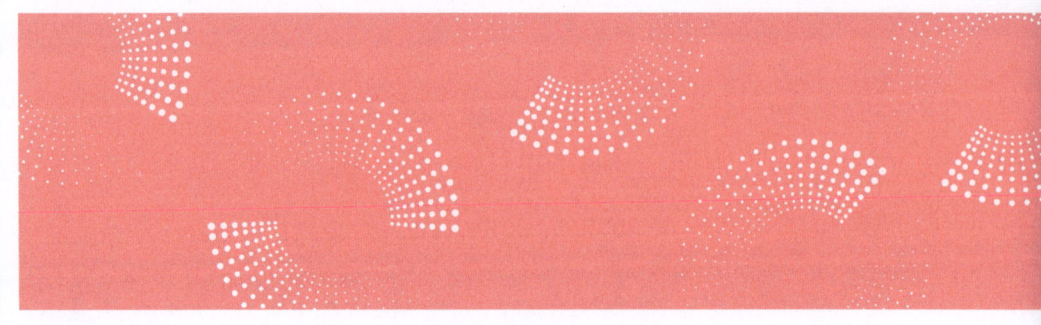

You can find peace by walking through the paper walls of fear.

Nobody was born anxious. Anxiety is something we learn, and need to unlearn in order to find peace.

I began by doing physical yoga, initially just for the workout, as exercise. I would get peaceful and calm at the end of it, and I was curious about that.

Mariel Hemmingway

Everybody's definition of tranquillity is different, so you will only really know it when you feel it.

No matter where you are, a sense of calm is closer than you think.

Though we often lose touch with tranquillity, it never loses touch with us.

Don't concentrate on your faults but on how you can improve. Small, gradual improvements pave the way to inner peace.

Being quiet and meditating on sound is something completely different and will be discovered very soon by a lot of people who feel that the visual world doesn't reach their soul anymore.

Karlheinz Stockhausen

The reason it seems hard to find calm is not because it is rare but because it is difficult to recognize.

I have never appreciated a quiet moment with a friend as much as a quiet moment with a book and I think part of that is my obsession with being older and time going faster and it's become increasingly sweeter for me.

Candice Bergen

Gently massage your temples with your fingers whenever you feel stress getting the better of you.

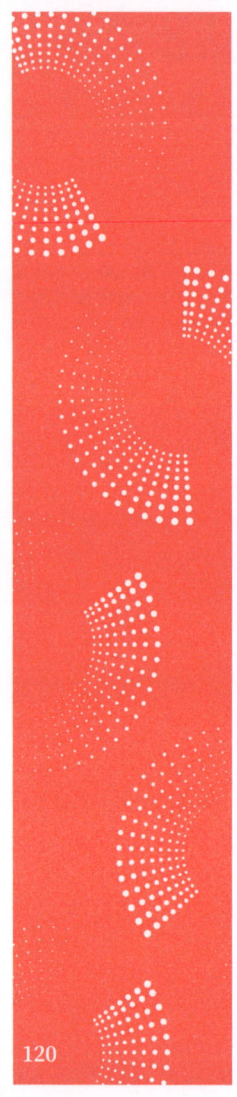

Once a week, turn off every electrical appliance and rediscover what it is like to engage with the world using just your own senses.

Tranquillity does not have to be pure or perfect in order for you to enjoy it.

It's a good idea always to do something relaxing prior to making an important decision in your life.

Paulo Coelho

A sense of calm produces more energy than a sense of panic.

---○

I love that quiet time when nobody's up and the animals are all happy to see me.

Olivia Newton-John

---○

Demand nothing from life and life will reward you with the gift of tranquillity.

Be grateful for everything that life brings your way – even challenges and defeats. We often learn more about ourselves in adversity than we do when life is going well.

Sometimes you have to sacrifice a little ambition in order to gain a large amount of peace.

When was the last time you spent a quiet moment just doing nothing – just sitting and looking at the sea, or watching the wind blowing the tree limbs, or waves rippling on a pond, a flickering candle or children playing in the park?

Ralph Marston

Kick off your shoes whenever you can. If you can go barefoot, so much the better.

Time spent worrying is time that could be spent relaxing.

If you look for it,
tranquillity is
all around you,
all of the time.

Tranquillity is as brittle or as strong as you are.

Rest is not idleness, and to lie sometimes on the grass under trees on a summer's day, listening to the murmur of the water, or watching the clouds float across the sky, is by no means a waste of time.

John Lubbock

In reading, a lonely quiet concert is given to our minds; all our mental faculties will be present in this symphonic exaltation.

Stéphane Mallarmé

127

Calm of the Heart

It is often those that we care about most who cause the most turbulence in our lives. Here we look at how to find, and keep, calm within relationships.

Romance is tempestuous.
Love is calm.
Mason Cooley

If you fill your heart
with compassion then
you will find your mind
fills with tranquillity.

Everything in life is uncertain:
accept this and you will
ultimately feel more secure.

Walk away from confrontation and you will be walking towards tranquillity.

Fears feed fears; confidence breeds confidence.

To enjoy tranquillity you must have enough room in your heart for it, so empty your heart of hatred or any other negative feelings.

The heart can sometimes be deceived, but it never lies.

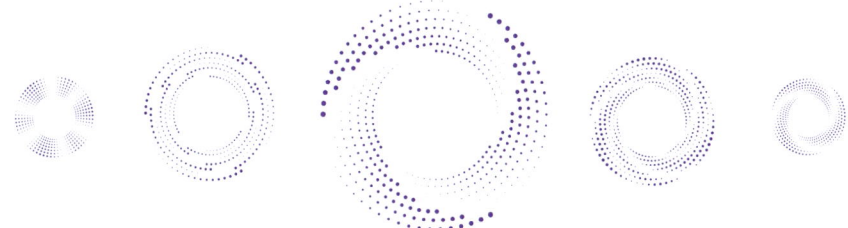

To understand others and to feel understood by them – that is tranquillity.

If we would build on a sure foundation in friendship, we must love friends for their sake rather than our own.
Charlotte Brontë

Occasionally a good cry helps release an enormous amount of tension.

If you are constantly suspicious of others you will always be tense.

Take your time over big decisions. Acting in haste often leads to trouble further down the line.

Saying 'thank you' regularly opens the door of tranquillity.

You must be in harmony with yourself before you can hope to be in harmony with the rest of the world.

It doesn't matter what the other is being, doing, having, saying, wanting, demanding. It doesn't matter what the other is thinking, expecting, planning. It only matters what you are being in relationship to that.

Neale Donald Walsch

Learn to trust,
and reward those who
trust in you, and you
will have all the calm
you desire.

Accepting that things do not always go according to plan will help you to relax when they don't.

Everything feels calmer by candlelight.

Follow the advice of those who have already found tranquillity.

Holding grudges hurts your peace of mind.

A kiss is a lovely trick designed by nature to stop speech when words become superfluous.

Ingrid Bergman

Tranquil people rarely interfere in the lives of others.

There is a sacredness in tears. They are not the mark of weakness, but of power. They speak more eloquently than ten thousand tongues. They are the messengers of overwhelming grief, of deep contrition, and of unspeakable love.

Washington Irving

Anyone can become angry – that is easy. But to be angry with the right person, to the right degree, at the right time, for the right purpose, and in the right way – this is not easy.

Aristotle

If you give in to everyone who makes demands upon your time then you will leave no time for you to be yourself.

A smile attracts other smiles, and smiles in turn attract tranquillity.

Speak in a soft voice and you will find yourself using soft words.

A kind heart is a fountain of gladness, making everything in its vicinity freshen into smiles.
Washington Irving

Take regular exercise and you'll feel better not just physically but emotionally too.

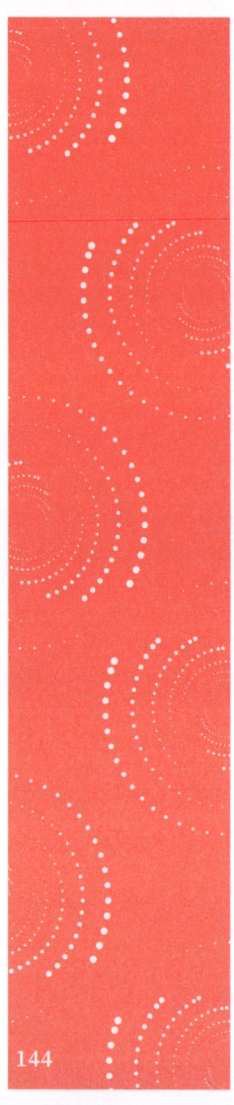

Sharing is sometimes more demanding than giving.

Mary Catherine Bateson

Buy less. It might feel like 'treating yourself' to buy things you don't need, but actually cluttering up your life with material things becomes a barrier to tranquillity after a while.

Phone a friend out of the blue just to see how they are.

Don't try and be perfect, and don't expect other people to be perfect either.

Apologize when you get something wrong. You'll feel better, and the person you apologize to will feel better too.

Civilization is a method of living and an attitude of equal respect for all people.

Jane Addams

Join a new group dedicated to a subject or pastime that interests you.

Have lunch with a friend. Eating 'on the go' is bad for digestion so make the time to eat properly.

Be calm in arguing; for fierceness makes error a fault, and truth discourtesy.
George Herbert

Be genuine, even if that means saying something you fear that others will not want to hear. You cannot find tranquillity by lying about who you are.

For there is no friend like
a sister in calm or stormy
weather; To cheer one on
the tedious way, to fetch
one if one goes astray, to lift
one if one totters down, to
strengthen whilst one stands.

Christina Rossetti

Give your loved ones space, and
create space for yourself too.

Don't feel sorry for yourself: 99% of feeling tranquil is not about what happens to you, but how you react to what happens to you.

Keep in regular contact with those you care about, even if it is only by text message.

Become a volunteer: helping others will make you feel good about yourself and you'll also make new friends.

I'll tell you what hermits realize. If you go off into a far, far forest and get very quiet, you'll come to understand that you're connected with everything.

Alan Watts

Always make eye contact when you're talking with somebody. They will relax if they feel you are interested in what they have to say, and this in turn will relax you.

In every group of friends, there is always one who tends to initiate get-togethers. Consider being that person for your group of friends.

If you have only one smile in you, give it to the people you love. Don't be surly at home, then go out in the street and start grinning 'Good morning' at total strangers.

Maya Angelou

When you enjoy somebody's company, make sure that they know it. Send a thank you card or just give them a quick call to say how much you enjoyed meeting up with them.

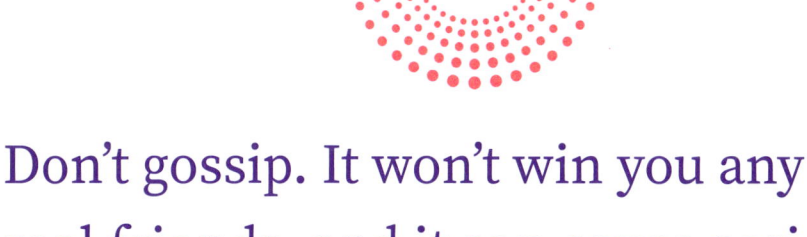

Don't gossip. It won't win you any real friends, and it can cause serious conflicts further down the line.

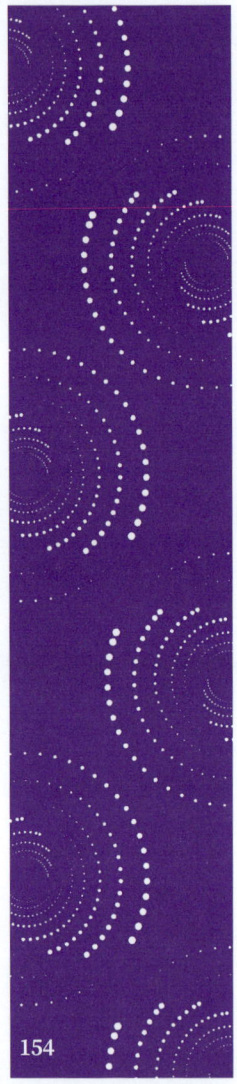

No person is your friend who demands your silence, or denies your right to grow.
Alice Walker

Learn how to keep a secret. A friend will not forgive you if something they tell you in confidence later becomes public knowledge.

One important reason to stay calm is that calm parents hear more. Low-key, accepting parents are the ones whose children keep talking.

Mary Pipher

Allow your loved ones to help you. It is good to be independent, but relationships are about give and take.

Don't forget old friends
when you acquire exciting new
ones. If you're loyal you will
receive loyalty in return
and this will help you feel
supported in times of trouble.

Try not to blur
the boundaries between
friends and lovers,
or you may end up
losing both a friend
and a lover.

Learn to be quiet enough to hear the genuine within yourself so that you can hear it in others.

Marian Wright Edelman

Making friends online can be a great comfort, but always remember to value your 'real' relationships too.

Don't harbour grudges: to be tranquil you must learn to forgive and forget.

Be there for your friends and family when they need you, but be careful not to let them crowd out your own life.

You see much more of your children once they leave home.
Lucille Ball

Sometimes you have to walk away from someone you love in order to find tranquillity, and you shouldn't feel guilty for doing so.

There's a magical tie to the land of our home, which the heart cannot break, though the footsteps may roam.

Eliza Cook

Warm your pajamas – and those of any loved ones you live with – before retiring to bed.

An arm around the shoulder at the right time is one of the quickest paths to tranquillity.

True love means accepting that people change – and embracing that change rather than trying to prevent it.

I've deliberately tried to calm myself down because eventually I want to be a good role model to my kids.

Robbie Williams

Slip a nice little note or treat into a friend's pocket when they're not looking.

Vows made in storms are forgotten in calm.

Thomas Fuller

Make at least one evening a week a TV-free evening.

Infatuation leads to feelings of insecurity. True love leads to a sense of calm.

There are times when silence has the loudest voice.

Leroy Brownlow

Self-love, my liege, is not so vile a sin as self-neglecting.
William Shakespeare

In love there are no shortcuts.

Romantics are calmer than cynics.

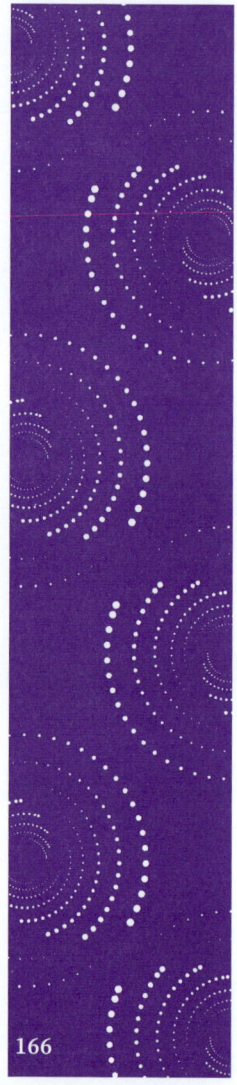

I inherited that calm from my father, who was a farmer. You sow, you wait for good or bad weather, you harvest, but working is something you always need to do. *Miguel Indurain*

In matters of the heart we are all amateurs, but if the only mistakes you make are genuine mistakes, you will always be forgiven by someone who truly loves you.

Good communication is vital in achieving tranquillity.

Show me the books he loves and I shall know the man far better than through mortal friends.

Dawn Adams

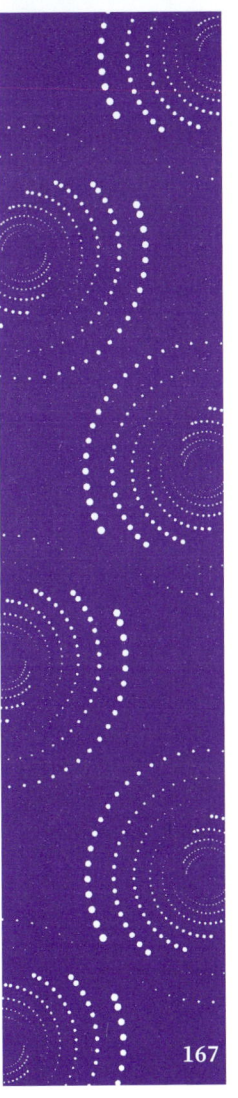

Don't dream of happy endings; work at making your relationships happy journeys.

Those who care about you are not mind-readers, so make sure they know what they can do to help you.

Always give 100%, but never expect 100% in return.

Journey with me to a true commitment to our environment. Journey with me to the serenity of leaving to our children a planet in equilibrium.

Paul Tsongas

If you're talkative by nature, make a conscious effort to listen more. If you're quiet by nature, make a conscious effort to open up a little more.

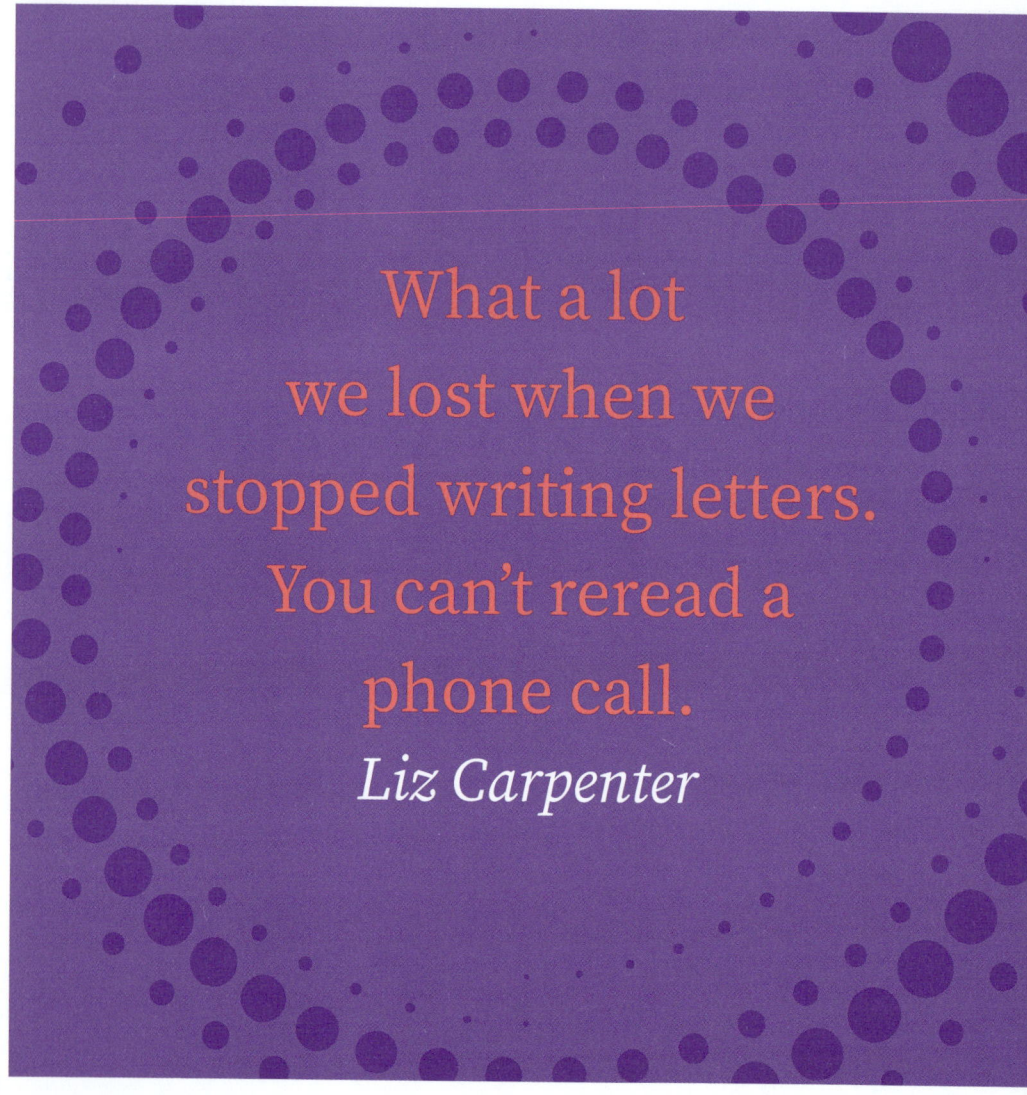

What a lot
we lost when we
stopped writing letters.
You can't reread a
phone call.
Liz Carpenter

Routine is boring rather than calming. Be spontaneous.

Note down special occasions and anniversaries in your diary, and make the time to celebrate them.

Silence is the true friend that never betrays.

Confucius

Be prepared to make sacrifices for your loved ones, but don't allow yourself to become a martyr.

Engagements with friends are as important as business meetings, so treat them accordingly.

Before, I was so stupid. But, you know, when you have friends who died on the street, you say, okay, let's calm down. It's not the kind of energy I want to have in life. I want to go slower, and longer.

Olivier Martinez

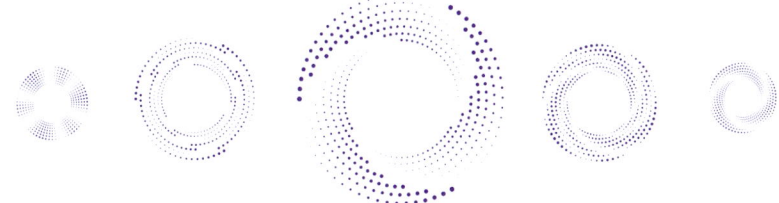

Don't try and pack all of your 'special time' into weekends. Try and find small amounts of tranquillity in each and every day.

Don't try and
'play it cool'.
Be honest and
open, and accept
that what will
be will be.

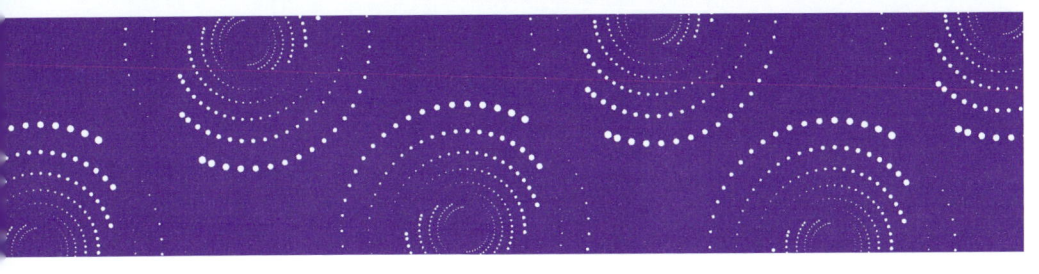

It is great to feel comfortable in a relationship, but never let yourself get so comfortable that you start to take your partner for granted.

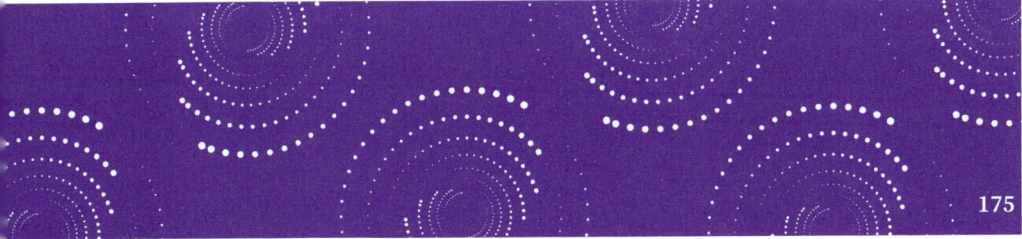

The seas are quiet when the winds give o'er; So calm are we when passions are no more!
Edmund Waller

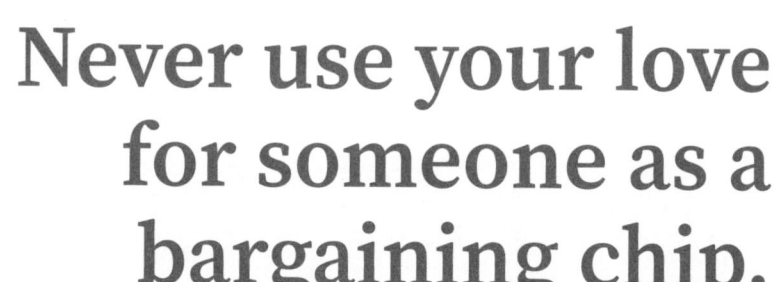

Never use your love for someone as a bargaining chip.

Make a 'keepsake box' and fill it with reminders of happy times you have shared with your loved ones.

Never gloat when you are right, or sulk when you are wrong.

Love is the emblem of eternity; it confounds all notions of time; effaces all memory of beginning, all fear of an end.
Germaine de Staël

It is not enough to simply tell yourself that your friends and family are
your number 1 priority: your actions have to reflect this. Work overtime in
your personal life and you'll be rewarded not with money but with harmony.

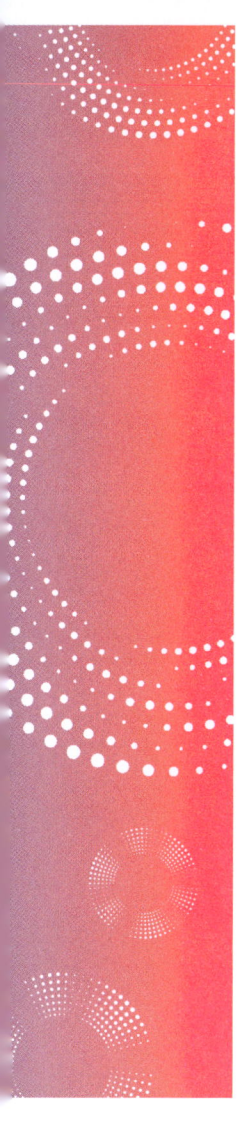

In relationships, there is no tranquillity without equality.

Silences make the real conversations between friends. Not the saying but the never needing to say is what counts.
Margaret Lee Runbeck

Love grows if you nurture it, and withers if you do not.

179

Re-read a book or re-watch a film you loved the first time.

I love children: especially when they cry, for then someone takes them away.

Nancy Mitford

Sharing a delicious meal together is both relaxing and intimate. Find the time to eat together.

Children learn by example: don't tell them to do one thing and then do another thing yourself.

Your days are short here; this is the last of your springs. And now in the serenity and quiet of this lovely place, touch the depths of truth, feel the hem of Heaven. You will go away with old, good friends. And don't forget when you leave why you came.
Adlai E. Stevenson

Cultivate solitude and quiet and a few sincere friends, rather than mob merriment, noise and thousands of nodding acquaintances.
William Powell

Act upon your feelings. Love is an emotion; romance is an action.

When all else is lost, the future still remains.

Christian Bovee

Small, genuine gestures are more meaningful than grand gestures that you feel obliged to make.

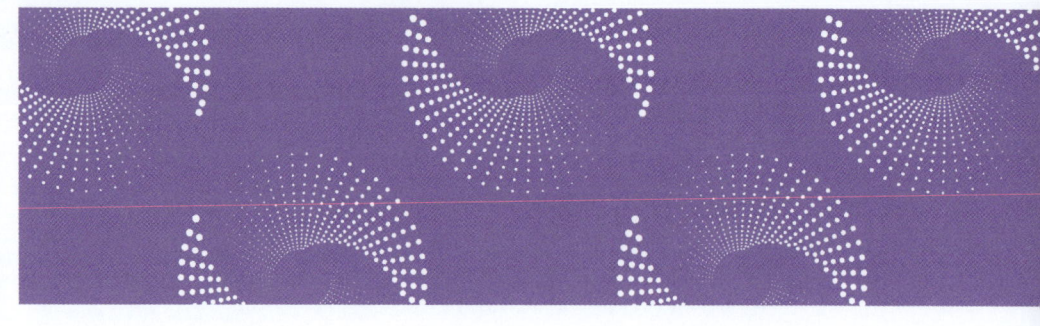

Allow your bedroom to be a place for romance and sleeping – and nothing else.

Take an afternoon off to go to the cinema.

Hugs cost nothing, so be generous in giving them to others.

Nothing feels quite as relaxing or indulgent as breakfast in bed.

Animals are such agreeable friends – they ask no questions, they pass no criticisms.
George Eliot

Emails and texts are convenient, but nothing tells someone you care like a letter does.

People do not
commit to one another
when they cease to have
any doubts; they commit
to one another when love
overcomes their doubts.

After a storm comes a calm.
Matthew Henry

Time with a loved one is the most precious time of all, so ensure that time cannot be interrupted.

In relationships, celebrate not just your similarities but your differences too.

There is a fellowship more quiet even than solitude, and which, rightly understood, is solitude made perfect.

Robert Louis Stevenson

No matter how close you are to others, make sure your very best friend is you.

There should always, always be time in your life for your loved ones.

It is easy to be calm when agreeing with someone, but much harder to be calm when disagreeing with someone.

Until I accept my faults I will most certainly doubt my virtues.
Hugh Prather

Calm at Work

Almost everybody feels under pressure in their workplace, so it is especially important to try and find calm moments amidst the daily grind.

Delegate whenever you can. You will place less pressure on yourself, and others will relish the faith you have placed in them.

Don't be tempted to use coffee as a 'pick-me-up' during the day.

[People] for the sake of getting a living forget to live. *Margaret Fuller*

Don't be tempted to use alcohol to 'wind down' after a hard day.

One of the symptoms of an approaching nervous breakdown is the belief that one's work is terribly important.

Bertrand Russell

Try taking exercise in your lunch hour, even if it is only a walk around the block.

Place soothing reminders of what you love around your workspace.

The pursuit, even of the best things, ought to be calm and tranquil.

Marcus Tullius Cicero

Set yourself
achievable goals
each day, and
celebrate when you
meet your targets.

The more tranquil a man
becomes, the greater
is his success, his influence,
his power for good. Calmness
of mind is one of the beautiful
jewels of wisdom.

James Allen

We all tend to 'over-breathe' when anxious, which only makes the symptoms of anxiety worse. Breathe in through your nose whilst counting to 3, then breathe out through your mouth whilst counting to 3. Continue breathing this way for 5 minutes and you are likely to feel calmer.

The more realistic your dreams the fewer your nightmares.

Change out of your work clothes as soon as you finish work.

Sometimes it's important to work for that pot of gold. But other times it's essential to take time off and to make sure that your most important decision in the day simply consists of choosing which colour to slide down on the rainbow.

Douglas Pagels

There's an hysterical, tired sense of humor that comes after working 14 hours a day, six days a week. I like those things because they take the pressure off the constant stress.

Tom Berenger

There is precious little hope to be got out of whatever keeps us industrious, but there is a chance for us whenever we cease work and become stargazers.

H. M. Tomlinson

Consider working flexi-time, if you can, and break up your day to add in calmer moments.

Make sure your workspace is adequately lit, but not harshly lit.

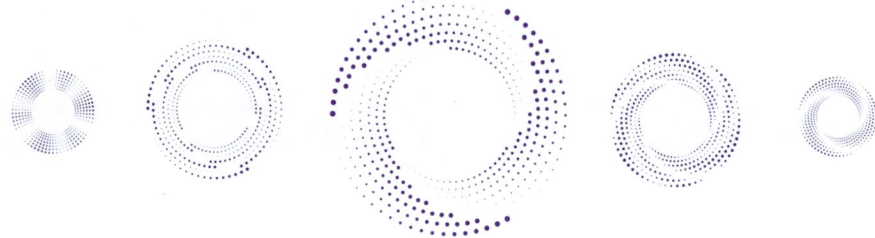

Follow effective action with quiet reflection. From the quiet reflection will come even more effective action.

Peter Drucker

Listen to relaxing music
during your work breaks.

Count to ten when
things get on top of you.
You are six times more
likely to suffer from
heart disease if you are
persistently angry.

Being in control of your life and having realistic expectations about your day-to-day challenges are the keys to stress management, which is perhaps the most important ingredient to living a happy, healthy and rewarding life.

Marilu Henner

Try not to take anything said to you in the workplace personally.

If we have not quiet in our minds,
outward comfort will do no more for us
than a golden slipper on a gouty foot.

John Bunyan

The only liberty an inferior man really cherishes is the liberty to quit work, stretch out in the sun, and scratch himself.

H. L. Mencken

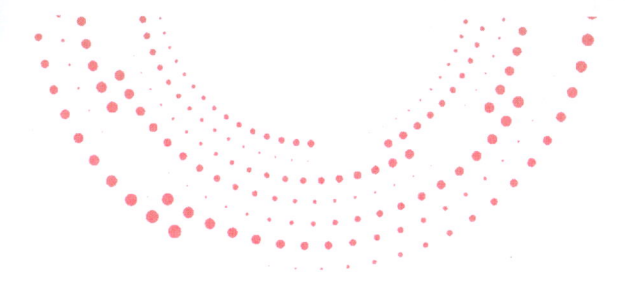

If you have done your best then you should be satisfied, regardless of whether a particular project you were working on succeeded or failed.

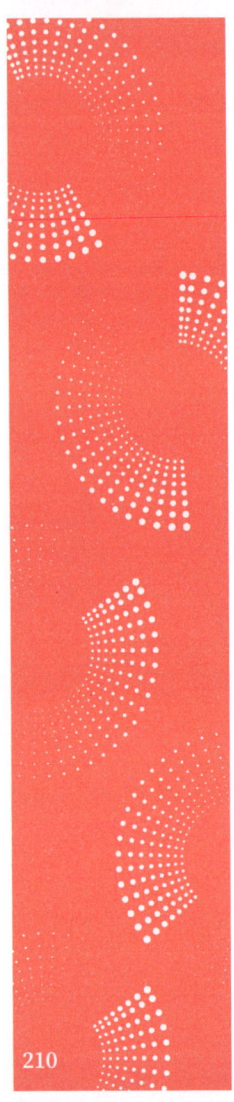

Set peace as your highest goal, and organize your life around it.

Brian Tracy

Focus on the possibilities of the future rather than worrying about the challenges it might bring.

If you can't pay for a thing, don't buy it. If you can't get paid for it, don't sell it. Do this, and you will have calm and drowsy nights, with all of the good business you have now and none of the bad. If you have time, don't wait for time.

Ernst Fischer

Try and talk to colleagues in person rather than sending emails or phoning them.

Have confidence in your own ability and difficulties will seem much smaller to you.

Don't just see opportunities, seize them.

I love deadlines.
I like the whooshing sound
they make as they fly by.

Douglas Adams

Enthusiasm leads
to success: success
leads to happiness
and happiness leads
to tranquillity.

Recognize the early signs of stress and act upon them to prevent them overwhelming you.

If you feel work is getting you down, remind yourself what you are working for. Focusing on the rewards that work brings, rather than work itself, often helps to put things in perspective.

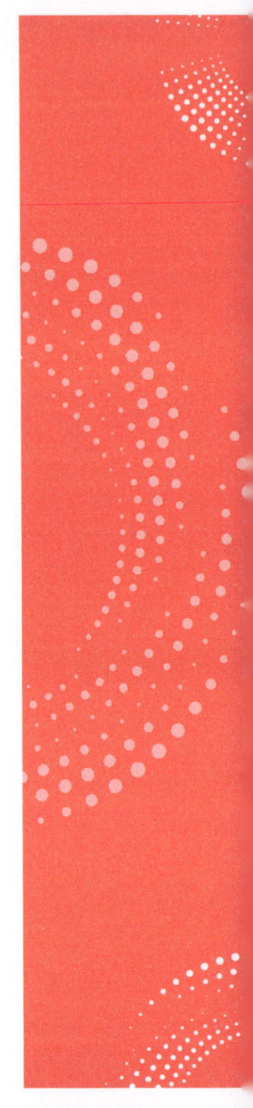

I have always been very calm on the outside. I'm not too stressed now just because I'm in Formula One. For me, tomorrow will be another day whether I finish first or last. I have to do the maximum and I cannot ask any more from myself.

Fernando Alonso

Don't bring your work home with you.

We live longer than our forefathers; but we suffer more from a thousand artificial anxieties and cares. They fatigued only the muscles; we exhaust the finer strength of the nerves.

Edward George Bulwer-Lytton

Taking a break is not the same as quitting.

Do things well, even if you are on a tight schedule. If you rush jobs you will end up having to do them again eventually.

Don't over-do it at Christmas parties, even if your colleagues are going wild. A single evening can cause embarrassment and stress for years.

The most powerful and respected leaders are those who can remain calm under pressure.

A life spent in constant labour is a life wasted, save a man be such a fool as to regard a fulsome obituary notice as ample reward.

George Jean Nathan

Success at work is worth nothing if it comes at the expense of happiness at home.

It does not matter how slowly you go, so long as you do not stop.
Confucius

Try not to travel in rush hour. Nothing is as frustrating as sitting in traffic.

Don't fall to pieces just because you're under a little pressure. Pressure is what turns coal into diamonds.

Now and then, bring treats into work and share them with your colleagues.

Put work out of your mind when you are at home. You will be more productive if you come at problems fresh rather than constantly turning them over in your mind.

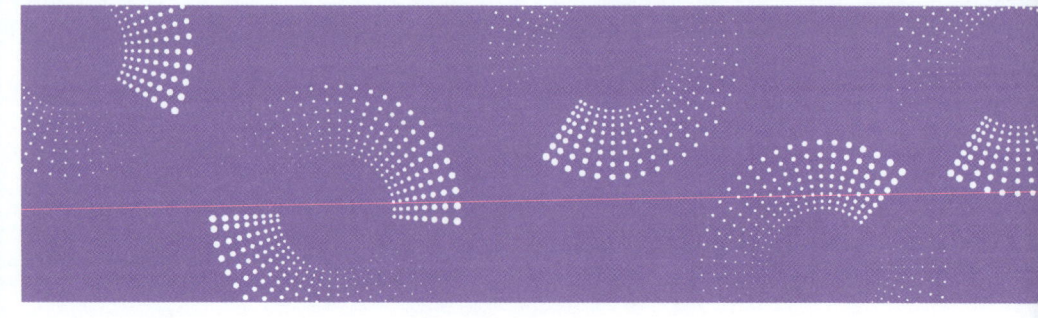

What isn't tried won't work.

Claude McDonald

Work is important, but it should never be your whole life. Remind yourself every day of the life you have outside of work.

Nothing in the world can take the place of persistence. Talent will not; nothing is more common than unsuccessful men with talent. Genius will not; unrewarded genius is almost a proverb. Education will not; the world is full of educated derelicts. Persistence and determination alone are omnipotent. The slogan 'press on' has solved and always will solve the problems of the human race.

Calvin Coolidge

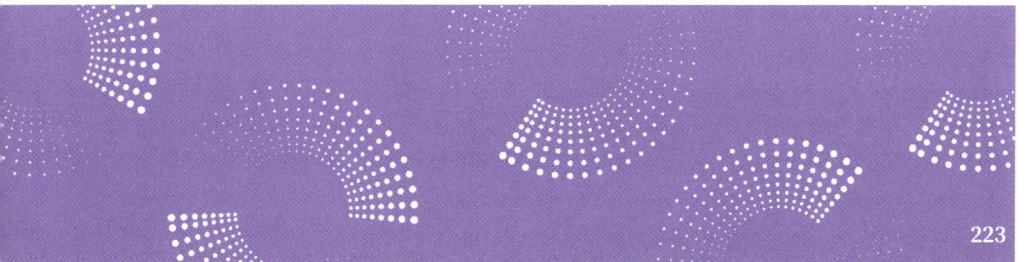

Calm of the Soul

There is little point journeying to remote idyllic places if we take our troubles with us. How do we find that true, deep, inner peace that lies within us?

In quiet moments when you think about it, you recognize what is critically important in life and what isn't. Be wise and don't let good things crowd out those that are essential.
Richard G. Scott

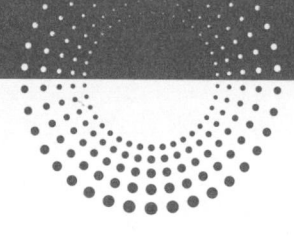

Tranquillity is the sense of feeling at one with the distant stars that gave birth to you.

Sometimes you have to turn off your mind in order to hear your soul whisper to you.

Only by much searching and mining are gold and diamonds obtained, and man can find every truth connected with his being if he will dig deep into the mine of his soul.

James Allen

If you treat every day as a precious gift it is almost impossible not to feel calm.

Listen to the birds singing at dawn and imagine they are singing to encourage you to make the very best of your day.

Peace starts with letting go. Remember that sometimes you have to un-learn bad old habits before you can develop good new habits.

To feel tranquillity you must learn to listen when the universe speaks.

Before you try and change the world, try changing the way you see the world.

The world renews itself every day, and, if you allow it to, then it can renew your soul every day too.

Always be punctual and you will avoid getting off on the wrong foot with people.

Yesterday is gone.
Tomorrow has not yet come.
We have only today. Let us begin.

Mother Teresa

Sometimes hanging on in there is all you need to do.

Seeking out quiet places helps, but, in the end, all peace, harmony and tranquillity come from within.

Not merely an absence of noise, Real Silence begins when a reasonable being withdraws from the noise in order to find peace and order in his inner sanctuary.
Peter Minard

Seen from space, planet Earth appears fragile, beautiful and calm. Keep this image in your mind when you are feeling stressed and frustrated.

Embrace change. You cannot grow without changing.

Bad things will happen from time to time, but you will only ever become a victim if you first choose to see yourself as one.

Make leaving the world a better place your only goal.

Lives are changed by a moment's listening to conscience, by a single and quiet inclination of the mind.

George A. Smith

Taking the easy option rarely leads to peace.

If you only ever focus on ever focus on surviving you will leave no time for living.

To find tranquillity you have to be ruthless in weeding out distractions.

Peace is not a relationship of nations. It is a condition of mind brought about by a serenity of soul. Peace is not merely the absence of war. It is also a state of mind. Lasting peace can come only to peaceful people.

Jawaharlal Nehru

No job is more important than the job of finding inner peace.

Every day is a fresh start and a clean slate.

It suddenly struck me that that tiny pea, pretty and blue, was the Earth. I put up my thumb and shut one eye, and my thumb blotted out the planet Earth. I didn't feel like a giant. I felt very, very small.

Neil Armstrong

Learn to get in touch with the silence within yourself and know that everything in this life has a purpose.

Elisabeth Kübler-Ross

Confronting problems causes them to shrink; ignoring problems causes them to grow.

If you value yourself you will take better care of yourself.

When Mozart was composing at the end of the eighteenth century, the city of Vienna was so quiet that fire alarms could be given verbally, by a shouting watchman mounted on top of St Stefan's Cathedral. In twentieth-century society, the noise level is such that it keeps knocking our bodies out of tune and out of their natural rhythms. This ever–increasing assault of sound upon our ears, minds, and bodies adds to the stress load of civilized beings trying to live in a highly complex environment.

Steven Halpern

Often we do not see the real world, but the reflection of ourselves in the world.

By all means be self-critical, but remember to praise yourself sometimes too.

We find the answers to life by living, not by thinking.

For no art and no religion is possible until we make allowances, until we manage to keep quiet the *enfant terrible* of logic that plays havoc with the other faculties.

John C. Ransom

There is no one meaning to life; we each have to find our own meaning.

Contemplating problems is not the same as worrying: learn to tell the difference.

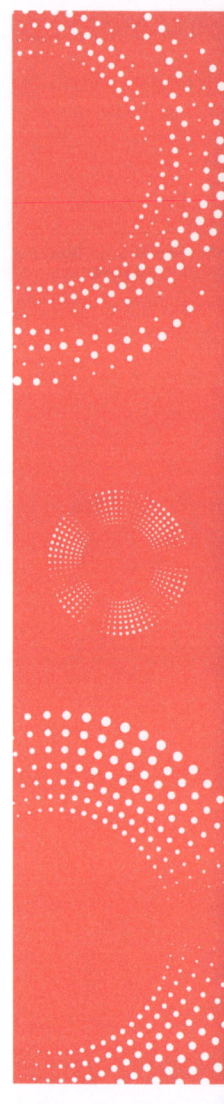

Words, words, words! They shut one off from the universe. Three quarters of the time one's never in contact with things, only with the beastly words that stand for them.
Aldous Huxley

Heaven and hell are not above and below us. We carry them in our hearts.

The Taoist Chuang Tzu once dreamt he was a butterfly, and then upon awaking wondered if he was actually a butterfly who was dreaming of being a man. We all build our own worlds in our minds, so make sure your mind is full of positive thoughts.

Tranquillity is about expanding into, not shrinking from, the universe that you are a part of.

Don't fall into the trap of thinking you don't have time to stop and relax. The busier you are the more important finding moments of calm becomes.

It is useless to force the rhythms of life. If I live with the anxiety to go fast, I will not live well. My addiction to speed will make me sick. The art of living is about learning how to give time to each and every thing. If I have sacrificed my life to speed, then that is impossible. Ultimately, slow means to take the time to reflect.
It means to take the time to think.
With calm, you arrive everywhere.

Carlos Petrini

Tranquillity is everywhere for those who are receptive to it.

The most important things in life are beyond language or explanation.

The components of anxiety, stress, fear, and anger do not exist independently of you in the world. They simply do not exist in the physical world, even though we talk about them as if they do.

Wayne Dyer

Tranquillity is found when you stop searching for it.

In our desire to find answers, we often make simple things more complicated than they need to be.

The material world is not life, but only one part of life.

Quietude, which some men cannot abide because it reveals their inward poverty, is as a palace of cedar to the wise, for along its hallowed courts the King in his beauty deigns to walk.
Charles H. Spurgeon

Now is always the time to tell yourself that here is where you belong.

The power of the imagination allows us to float along a gentle stream even when we are riding a bus through a busy city.

We only know what courage is because of the challenges that sometimes require us to find it.

249

Take control of your thoughts rather than letting your thoughts control you.

You cannot perceive beauty, but with a serene mind.

Henry David Thoreau

Every single person you meet can teach you something about yourself.

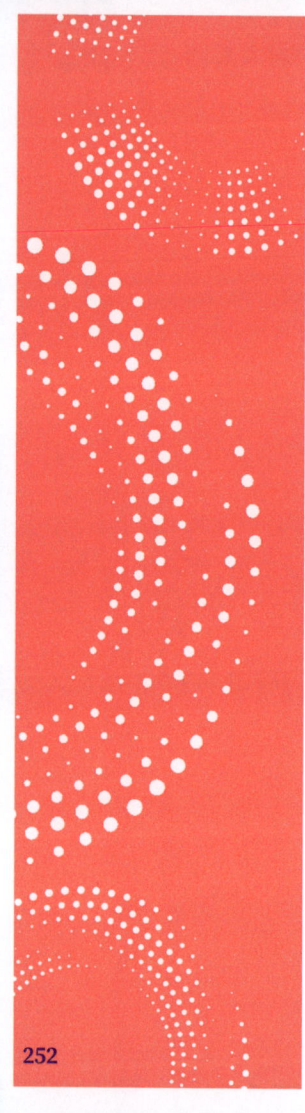

With an eye made quiet by the power of harmony, and the deep power of joy, we see into the life of things.
William Wordsworth

Listen to the opinions of others, but never let them override your own judgement.

Nobody is perfect, thank goodness.

There is a theory which states that if ever anyone discovers exactly what the Universe is for and why it is here, it will instantly disappear and be replaced by something even more bizarre and inexplicable. There is another theory which states that this has already happened.

Douglas Adams

Be kind. Whatever you do to others is ultimately what you do to yourself.

To see things in the seed, that is genius.
Lao Tzu

Serenity cannot be seen, heard or touched, yet it lies waiting for us within everything we see, hear and touch.

Never take tranquillity for granted. Store it within your heart so that you can tap into it when you most need it.

Calm doesn't come easily – it requires commitment, dedication and practice.

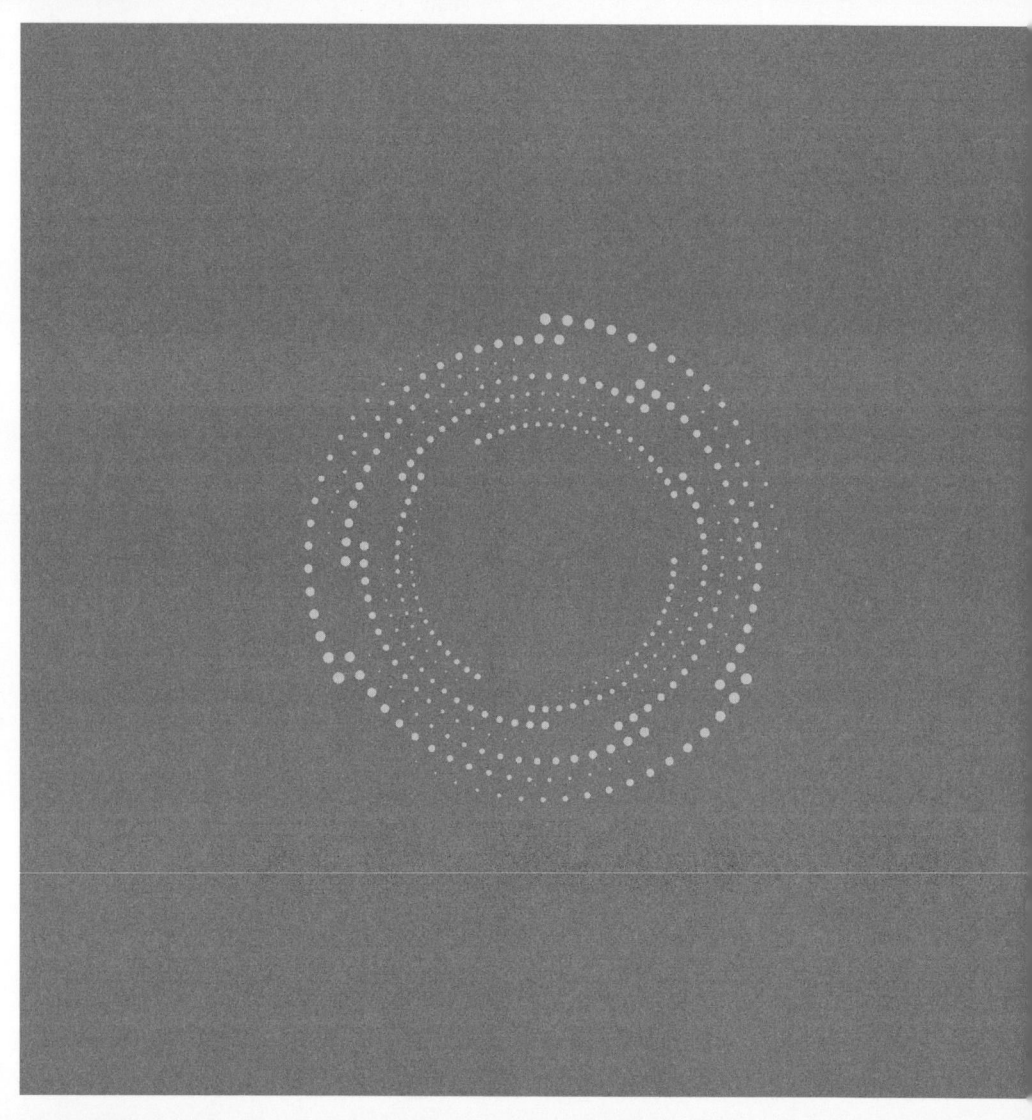

Calm Lives

Why does it seem like such a challenge to retain a sense of calm in the course of daily life? Thinking about what induces serenity in you may be the start of reversing this.

Retire into yourself as much as possible.

Seneca

Of any stopping place in life, it is good to ask whether it will be a good place from which to go on as well as a good place to remain.

Mary Catherine Bateson

The field of consciousness is tiny. It accepts only one problem at a time.

Antoine de Saint-Exupéry

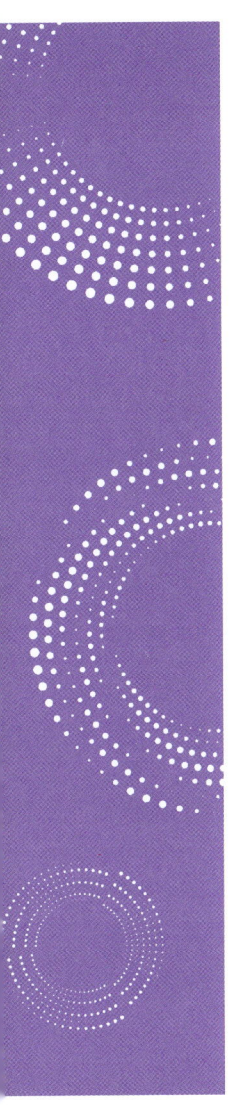

Great events make me quiet and calm; it is only trifles that irritate my nerves.

Queen Victoria

The life of inner peace, being harmonious and without stress, is the easiest type of existence.

Norman Vincent Peale

Take the time to listen and absorb your thoughts about what you hear. Active listening is at the heart of a tranquil response to life.

Accustomed to the veneer of noise,
to the shibboleths of promotion,
public relations, and market research,
society is suspicious of those who
value silence.

John Lahr

What I dream of is an art of balance, of
purity and serenity devoid of troubling or
depressing subject matter – a soothing,
calming influence on the mind, rather like
a good armchair which provides relaxation
from physical fatigue.

Henri Matisse

I'm not afraid of storms, for I'm learning to sail my ship.
Louisa May Alcott

The best cure for the body is a quiet mind.
Napoléon Bonaparte

Few things are brought to a successful issue by impetuous desire, but most by calm and prudent forethought.
Thucydides

The world is never quiet, even its silence eternally resounds with the same notes, in vibrations which escape our ears. As for those that we perceive, they carry sounds to us, occasionally a chord, never a melody.

Albert Camus

Time is a dressmaker specializing in alterations.

Faith Baldwin

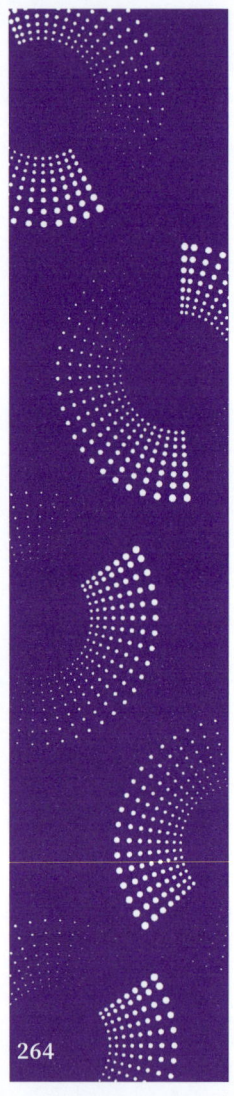

The talkative parrot is shut up in a cage. Other birds, without speech, fly freely about.
Saskya Pandita

He who is of calm and happy nature will hardly feel the pressure of age, but to him who is of an opposite disposition youth and age are equally a burden.
Plato

You grow up the day you have your first real laugh at yourself.

Ethel Barrymore

It is always calming to return to the breath. If you find yourself getting stressed, check that your breathing hasn't become shallower.

If a man will begin with certainties, he shall end in doubts, but if he will be content to begin with doubts, he shall end in certainties.
Francis Bacon

Talk that does not end in any kind of action is better suppressed altogether.
Thomas Carlyle

The fragrance always stays in the hand that gives the rose.
Hada Bejar

It was only from an inner calm that man was able to discover and shape calm surroundings.
Stephen Gardiner

Nothing is more useful than silence.
Menander of Athens

Many a calm river begins as a turbulent waterfall, yet none hurtles and foams all the way to the sea.

Mikhail Lermontov

Our faith in the present dies out long before our faith in the future.

Ruth Benedict

Try to keep opinions to a minimum when considering factual information about the world at large.

Happiness is good health and a bad memory.
Ingrid Bergman

He who seldom speaks, and with one calm, well-timed word can strike dumb the loquacious, is a genius or a hero.
Johann Kaspar Lavater

Everybody needs beauty as well as bread, places to play in and pray in, where nature may heal and give strength to body and soul.
John Muir

The good and the wise lead quiet lives.
Euripides

Certainty is the mother of quiet and repose, and uncertainty the cause of variance and contentions.

Edward Coke

Birds sing after a storm; why shouldn't people feel as free to delight in whatever sunlight remains to them?

Rose Kennedy

People are never quiet. It's go, go, go. I'm a go-getter, but you need rest and silence, just to sit around and think about things.

Dana Hill

In struggling against anguish one never produces serenity; the struggle against anguish only produces new forms of anguish.

Simone Weil

Cows are amongst the gentlest of breathing creatures; none show more passionate tenderness to their young when deprived of them; and, in short, I am not ashamed to profess a deep love for these quiet creatures.

Thomas de Quincey

The brain is not, and cannot be, the sole or complete organ of thought and feeling. *Alice Stone Blackwell*

Now all my teachers are dead except silence.

W. S. Merwin

Age is something that doesn't matter, unless you are a cheese. *Billie Burke*

Power is so characteristically calm, that calmness in itself has the aspect of strength.

Edward George Bulwer-Lytton

Sooner or later you learn that you belong in the big leagues, and that makes you calm down.

Dennis Eckersley

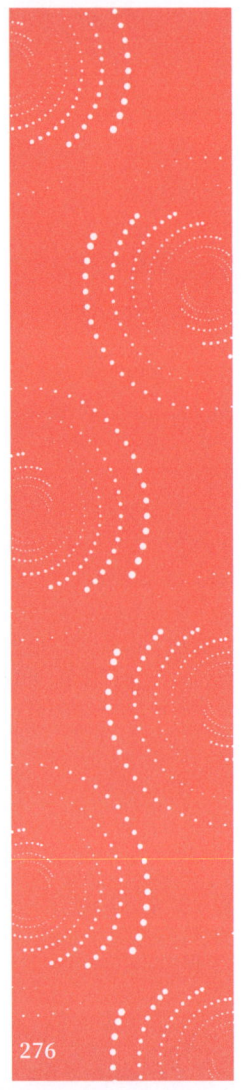

A garden must combine the poetic and the mysterious with a feeling of serenity and joy.
Luis Barragán

Remember the quiet wonders. The world has more need of them than it has for warriors.
Charles de Lint

The healthy being craves an occasional wildness, a jolt from normality, a sharpening of the edge of appetite, his own little festival of Saturnalia, a brief excursion from his way of life.
Robert Morrison MacIver

Don't engage in gossip. It does not promote calm or happiness in either yourself or in others. Think about how uncomfortable you feel after you've spent time with someone who likes to gossip.

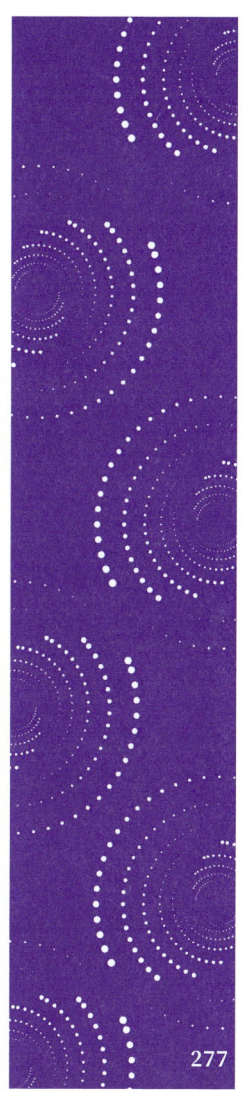

I moved to New York City for my health. I'm paranoid and New York was the only place where my fears were justified.
Anita Weiss

Life being very short, and the quiet hours of it few, we ought to waste none of them in reading valueless books.
John Ruskin

I don't think necessity is the mother of invention. Invention, in my opinion, arises directly from idleness, possibly also from laziness – to save oneself trouble.
Agatha Christie

The deepest rivers make least din, the silent soule doth most abound in care.
William Alexander

One's age should be tranquil, as childhood should be playful. Hard work at either extremity of life seems out of place. At midday the sun may burn, and men labour under it; but the morning and evening should be alike calm and cheerful.

Thomas Arnold

In this world without quiet corners, there can be no easy escapes from history, from hullabaloo, from terrible, unquiet fuss.

Salman Rushdie

Life is a mystery as deep as ever death can be.

Mary Mapes Dodge

Besides the noble art of getting things done, there is the noble art of leaving things undone. The wisdom of life consists in the elimination of non-essentials.
Lin Yutang

A wise man adapts himself to circumstances as water shapes itself to the vessel that contains it.
Chinese proverb

The poet is willing to stop anywhere... And it's that willingness to slow down and examine the mysterious bits of fluff in our lives that is the poet's interest.
William Collins

A poor life this if,
full of care,
We have no time to
stand and stare.
William Henry Davies

I sometimes suspect that half
our difficulties are imaginary
and that if we kept quiet about
them they would disappear.
Robert Lynd

Real joy comes not from ease or riches or from the praise of others, but from doing something worthwhile.

Wilfred Grenfell

Dream as if you'll live forever. Live as if you'll die today.

James Dean

Nothing is worth more than this day.

Johann Wolfgang von Goethe

The third-rate mind is only happy
when it is thinking with the majority.
The second-rate mind is only happy
when it is thinking with the minority.
The first-rate mind is only happy
when it is thinking.

A. A. Milne

What we think, or what we know,
or what we believe is, in the end, of little
consequence. The only consequence is
what we do.
John Ruskin

It's good to shut up sometimes.

Marcel Marceau

There is a great difference between worry and concern. A worried person sees a problem, and a concerned person solves a problem.

Harold Stephens

In quiet places, reason abounds.

Adlai E. Stevenson

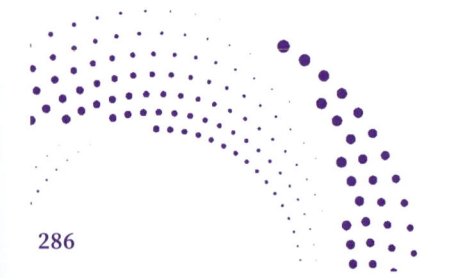

Everyone thinks of changing the world, but no one thinks of changing himself.

Leo Tolstoy

You don't have to have fought in a war to love peace.

Geraldine Ferraro

The language of excitement is at best picturesque merely. You must be calm before you can utter oracles.

Henry David Thoreau

I'm full of fears and I do my best to avoid difficulties and any kind of complications. I like everything around me to be clear as crystal and completely calm.

Alfred Hitchcock

Don't give in to despair. Even the worst of challenges must pass eventually.

At some point in life, the world's beauty becomes enough.

Toni Morrison

Throughout my life I'd learnt that when you're in the serious situations, you've got to try to stay calm. Because that's the way you get out of them.

John Newcombe

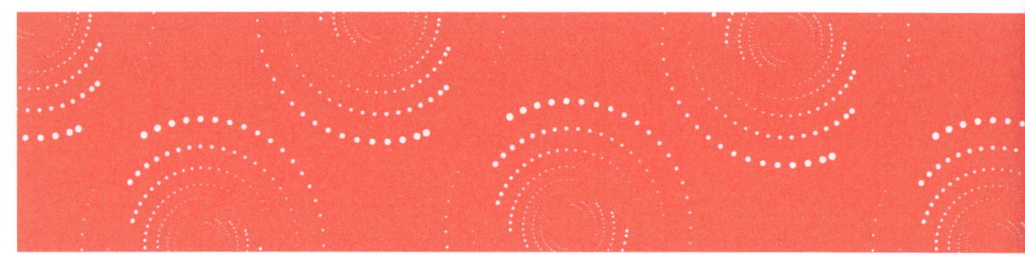

One of the most important lessons to learn is how to gracefully accept the things you can't change.

A happy life is just a string of happy moments. But most people don't allow the happy moment, because they're so busy trying to get a happy life.

Esther Hicks

There is only one way to happiness and that is to cease worrying about things which are beyond the power of our will.
Epictetus

I need something to do when I'm not working, or I crawl up the walls. So I've just taken up kung fu. I was looking for some kind of calming, relaxing activity. I tried yoga, but it wasn't really me.
Ian Hart

Climb the mountains and get their good tidings.
John Muir

Make your home a place of peace.

When a house is being built which is to be made as strong as possible, the building takes place in fine weather and in calm, so that nothing may hinder the structure from acquiring the needed solidity.

Origen

I like to sit back and take in nature. To look at the birds, listen to their singing, go hiking, camping and jogging and running, walking along the beach, playing games and sometimes being alone with the great outdoors. It's very special to me.

Larry Wilcox

What stresses you today will be forgotten very soon so why not forget it right away?

I don't know what my path is yet. I'm just walking on it.

Olivia Newton-John

I have learned silence from
the talkative, toleration from
the intolerant, and kindness
from the unkind; yet, strange,
I am ungrateful to those teachers.

Kahlil Gibran

When I can look life in the eyes, grown calm and very coldly wise, life will have given me the truth, and taken in exchange – my youth.
Sara Teasdale

All truly great thoughts are conceived by walking.
Friedrich Nietzsche

Silence is as deep as eternity; speech as shallow as time.

Thomas Carlyle

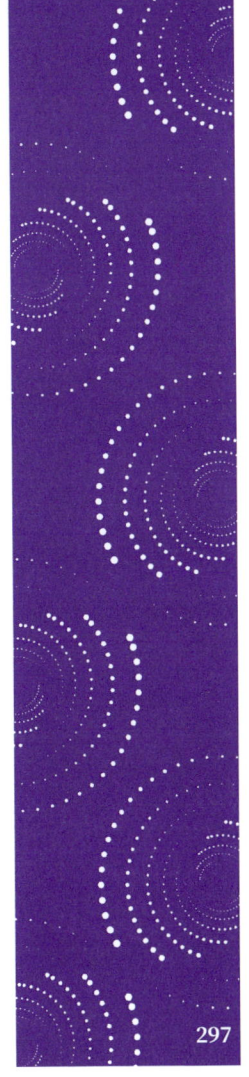

The moment one gives close attention to anything, even a blade of grass, it becomes a mysterious, awesome, indescribably magnificent world in itself.

Henry Miller

A liberal is a man or a woman or a child who looks forward to a better day, a more tranquil night, and a bright, infinite future.

Leonard Bernstein

I have often lamented that we cannot close our ears with as much ease as we can our eyes.

Richard Steele

In the midst of winter,
I found there was within
me an invincible summer.

Albert Camus

Fortunately, psychoanalysis is not the only way to resolve inner conflicts. Life itself remains a very effective therapist.
Karen Horney

Life's under no obligation to give us what we expect.

Margaret Mitchell

There are some things you learn best in calm, and some in storm.
Willa Cather

And this, our life, exempt from public haunt, finds tongues in trees, books in the running brooks, sermons in stones, and good in everything.
William Shakespeare

I can live with doubt and uncertainty and not knowing. I think it is much more interesting to live not knowing than to have answers that might be wrong.
Richard Feynman

The best translations cannot convey to us the strength and exquisite delicacy of thought in its native garb, and he to whom such books are shut flounders about in outer darkness.

Edwin Booth

Nobody sees a flower really, it is so small. We haven't time, and to see takes time – like to have a friend takes time.

Georgia O'Keeffe

Silence is a source of great strength.
Lao Tzu

I have tremendous faith in the universe. I feel at home on this planet. Even though it's a very big world out there, I plan on walking right through the middle of it unharmed.
Marion Ross

New York has a trip-hammer vitality which drives you insane with restlessness if you have no inner stabilizer.
Henry Miller

Happiness is the absence of striving for happiness.
Zhuangzi

I think that the ideal space must contain elements of magic, serenity, sorcery and mystery.

Luis Barragán

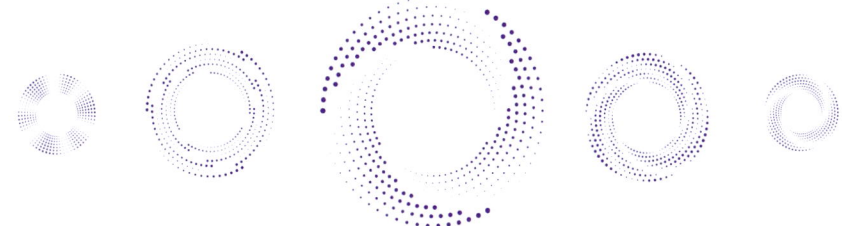

To be 'on edge,' you are literally not centred – not being in your spiritual centre.

Carrie Latet

The sole art that suits me is that which, rising from unrest, tends towards serenity.
André Gide

Take time to smell the roses. Pausing each day to appreciate beauty is the surest way to calm.

Trying to determine what is going on in the world by reading newspapers is like trying to tell the time by watching the second hand of a clock.

Ben Hecht

To play well you must feel tranquil and at peace. I have never been troubled by nerves in golf because I felt I had nothing to lose and everything to gain.

Harry Vardon

All the problems of the world can be solved in a garden.
Geoff Lawton

It is good to have an end to journey towards;
but it is the journey that matters in the end.
Ursula K. Le Guin

I like a very dark house, just black. I sit there and just think. Once I'm still and quiet inside, I'll begin. It's very personal; it has to be. One song may be Bach, the next blues, a song from TV, or a nursery rhyme or jazz piece.
Bobby McFerrin

Tranquil pleasures last the longest; we are not fitted to bear the burden of great joys.
Christian Nestell Bovee

We think a happy life consists in tranquillity of mind.

Marcus Tullius Cicero

Sometimes you need to pause for a relaxing bath or a good book... and that's okay to do.

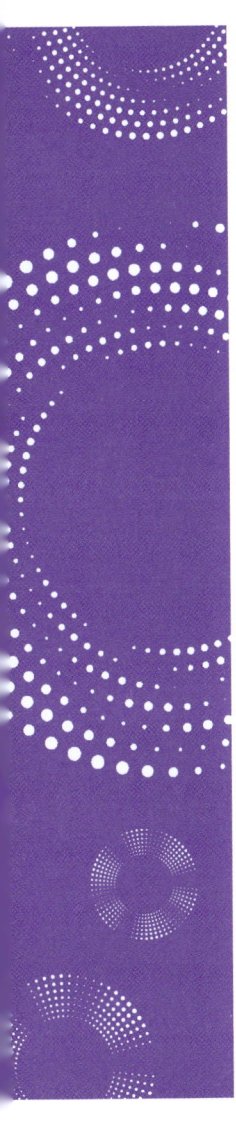

Almost all our faults are more pardonable than the methods we resort to to hide them.

François de La Rochefoucauld

Music itself is a great source of relaxation. Parts of it anyway. Working in the studio, that's not relaxing, but playing an instrument that I don't know how to play is unbelievably relaxing, because I don't have any pressure on me.

Jackson Browne

I know the joy
of fishes in the river
through my own joy,
as I go walking along
the same river.

Zhuangzi

Silence is the universal refuge, the sequel to all dull discourses and all foolish acts, a balm to our every chagrin, as welcome after satiety as after disappointment.

Henry David Thoreau

I'm not very good at relaxing. Reading's the main thing. On the bus, on the tube, on the loo. Literally all the time. I mean, I don't think there's a moment of the day when I wouldn't be if I was left alone.
Samuel West

Like water which can clearly mirror the sky and the trees only so long as its surface is undisturbed, the mind can only reflect the true image of the Self when it is tranquil and wholly relaxed.

Indra Devi

I need to go someplace faraway that doesn't have telephones and doesn't have a record player and doesn't have movie theaters and people walking down the street in order to not do anything.

Will Oldham

The most intense conflicts, if overcome, leave behind a sense of security and calm that is not easily disturbed. It is just these intense conflicts and their conflagration which are needed to produce valuable and lasting results.

Carl Jung

A mind at peace, a mind centred and not focused on harming others, is stronger than any physical force in the universe.
Wayne Dyer

A crust eaten in peace is better than a banquet partaken in anxiety.
Aesop

Ill fortune never crushed that man whom good fortune deceived not.
Francis Bacon

I do pottery. I love it. It's very relaxing; it takes me to another planet.

Eva Herzigová

Take a course in good water and air; and in the eternal youth of Nature you may renew your own. Go quietly, alone; no harm will befall you.

John Muir

I started walking at night with my sister-in-law which has been amazing. It really does something for you. It just kind of clears the mind, it just makes you feel better, things start to tighten a little bit.
Ashley Scott

Silence is a sounding thing, to one who listens hungrily.
Gwendolyn Bennett

An inability to stay quiet is one of the
most conspicuous failings of mankind.

Walter Bagehot

**All of us might wish at times
that we lived in a more
tranquil world, but we don't.
And if our times are difficult
and perplexing, so are they
challenging and filled with
opportunity.**

Robert Kennedy

Staying Calm

Tranquillity is notoriously fragile; it can be lost in the blink of an eye. So how do we protect our hard-won sense of calm, and how do we restore it if we lose it?

With increased opportunity comes increased stress. The stress comes from multiple conflicting demands and very little in the way of role models.
Madeline Hemmings

It is entirely natural to feel angry and frustrated sometimes. Indeed letting your anger out is the only way to restore your equilibrium.

When things go wrong, don't look for someone to blame. Spend your time making things right again instead.

Learn to forgive – both others and yourself.

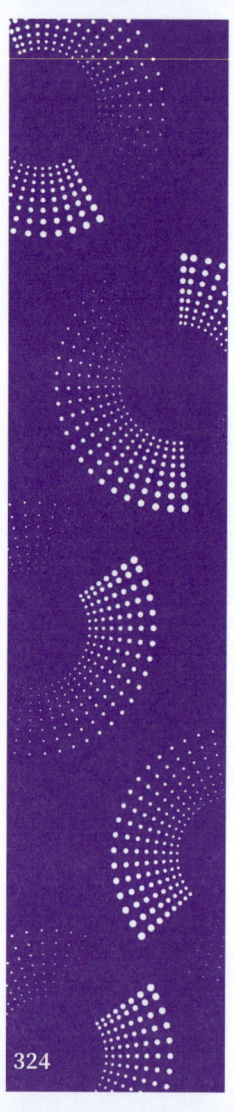

Retain your sense of humour.

Self-pity in its early stages is as snug as a feather mattress. Only when it hardens does it become uncomfortable.

Maya Angelou

Accept help when it is offered, but never depend entirely on someone else.

It is far better to try and fail than never to try at all.

Don't ignore the facts – change them.

It is when the situation is negative that a positive outlook is most useful.

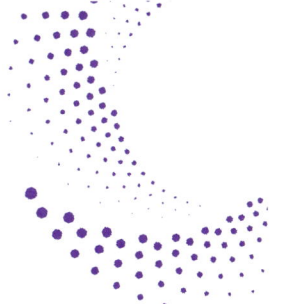

Aerodynamically the bumblebee shouldn't be able to fly, but the bumblebee doesn't know that so it goes on flying anyway.
Mary Kay Ash

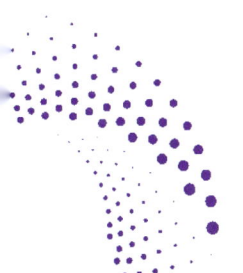

Offering encouragement to others often leads to you encouraging yourself too.

Keep looking towards the future. Nothing is as corrosive to tranquillity as regret.

Stress is basically a disconnection from the earth, a forgetting of the breath. Stress is an ignorant state. It believes that everything is an emergency. Nothing is that important. Just lie down.

Natalie Goldberg

Always hope for the best but plan for the worst.

No matter how big or soft or warm your bed is, you still have to get out of it.
Grace Slick

Don't be ashamed of failure: if you resolve to learn from your mistakes then failure can become your greatest teacher.

True friendships
are often forged
in the midst
of shared
adversity.

You can't please everyone all of the time.

Whenever you get down about how things are, focus on what things have the potential to become.

The best way to avenge those who harm you is to thrive.

Not a shred of evidence exists in favor of the idea that life is serious.
Brendan Gill

Accept that you don't always get what you deserve, at least in the short term.

It is when others doubt you that you most need faith in yourself.

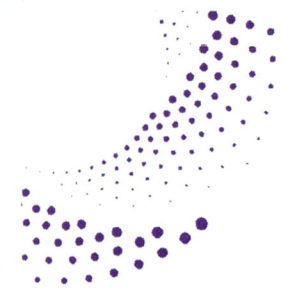

You cannot change the past, but you can learn from it to build a better future.

Courage is the price that life exacts for granting peace. The soul that knows it not, knows no release from little things; knows not the livid loneliness of fear.

Amelia Earhart

Don't retreat
into your shell just
because you have
had a setback.
Dust yourself down
and come
out fighting.

The rays of happiness,
like those of light,
are colourless when unbroken.

Henry W. Longfellow

Never underestimate your capacity to turn things around.

Be prepared to change your approach, but don't compromise on your values in order to get yourself out of a difficult situation.

Sometimes your best isn't good enough – but remember that all you can ever do is your best.

Within every challenge there is also a fresh opportunity.

Each day should have a clearly marked emergency exit sign.

Dr Sun Wolf

Lashing out at others when things go wrong only makes matters worse.

Your true friends will help you when things look bleak, so don't be too proud to turn to them.

339

If you never quit then you can never really lose.

The gem cannot be polished
without friction, nor man
be perfected without trials.
Danish proverb

Don't get angry with yourself. Calmly look at what you need to change about yourself in order to do better next time.

Keep the faith. You will only have lost everything when you have lost hope.

Don't be afraid to retrace your steps and try a different route.

When you feel lost, surround yourself with familiar things until you get your spiritual bearings again.

In times of life crisis, whether wild fires or smoldering stress, the first thing I do is go back to basics... am I eating right, am I getting enough sleep, am I getting some physical and mental exercise everyday?

Edward Albert

The world needs the rain just as much as it needs the sun.

I wonder what it is in the New York air that enables me to sit up till all hours of the night in an atmosphere which in London would make a horse dizzy, but here merely clears the brain.

James Agate

Never use alcohol or drugs as a crutch in times of trouble.

The more difficult your goals are to achieve, the more satisfying they will be when you ultimately achieve them.

There is a way to look at the past. Don't hide from it. It will not catch you if you don't repeat it.
Pearl Bailey

Nobody has all of the answers. Settle for asking the right questions.

You will never find out
who you really are unless
you are prepared to risk
failing at something.

Keep calm and carry on.

Wherever we look upon this earth, the opportunities take shape within the problems.

Nelson A. Rockefeller

Thinking negatively only makes problems worse.

Focus not on what you have lost but on what you still have.

Getting away from it all can give you a fresh perspective. Running away from it all will only bring more problems further down the line.

Everything that irritates us about others can lead us to an understanding of ourselves.

Carl Jung

No matter how great the problem you are facing, promise yourself you will not think about it after a certain time in the evening. Losing sleep through worrying will not help you or those around you.

Check your goals are realistic.
If you try and achieve the
impossible you will be
endlessly disappointed.

Being able to laugh at
ourselves is important.
A disaster is easier to cope with
if you can turn it into a farce.

Remember that you will never truly appreciate the highs of life unless you have also experienced the lows.

Tranquillity does not come when you feel successful, it comes when you feel satisfied: learn to tell the difference.

It's not stress that kills us, it is our reaction to it.
Hans Selye

Spend as much time in nature as you can. If you're feeling overwhelmed, go for a quick walk and drink in the greenery around you. It is a tonic that can't be beaten for efficacy.

The
Calm
Smile

Being able to laugh at life is key to unwinding. Kick off your shoes and enjoy the wit of those who have sought, found, and lost their calm throughout the ages.

If you ask what is the single most important key to longevity, I would have to say it is avoiding worry, stress and tension. And if you didn't ask me, I'd still have to say it.

George Burns

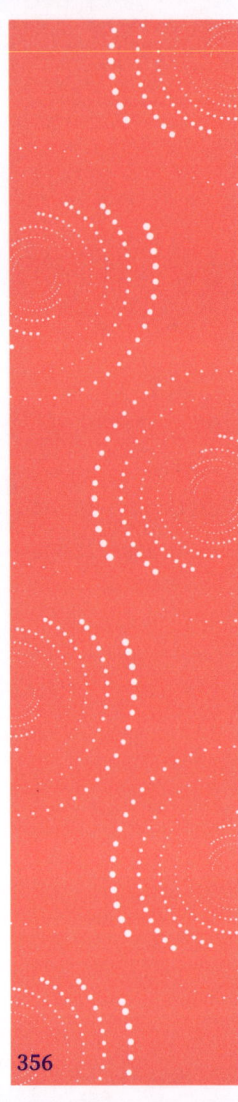

Reality is the leading cause of stress among those in touch with it.
Lily Tomlin

How beautiful it is to do nothing, and then to rest afterward.
Spanish proverb

The world is moving
so fast these days that the
one who says it can't
be done is generally
interrupted by
someone doing it.

Harry Emerson Fosdick

A vacation frequently means that the family goes away for a rest, accompanied by a mother who sees that the others get it.
Marcelene Cox

The object of opening the mind, as of opening the mouth, is to shut it again on something solid.
G. K. Chesterton

A bee is never as busy as it seems; it's just that it can't buzz any slower.
Kin Hubbard

Don't panic.

Douglas Adams

If people concentrated on the really important things in life, there'd be a shortage of fishing poles.

Doug Larson

I try to take one day at a time, but sometimes several days attack me at once.

Jennifer Yane

Death is nature's way of telling you to slow down.

There's never enough time to do all the nothing you want.

Bill Watterson

Are you a good role model for any children in your life?

Authors like cats because they are such quiet, lovable, wise creatures, and cats like authors for the same reasons.

Robertson Davies

I don't feel old. I don't feel anything until noon. Then it's time for my nap.

Bob Hope

I don't even butter my bread; I consider that cooking.

Katherine Cebrian

A good marriage is based on mutual respect, listening to each other, and knowing when your partner needs support – whether that's help with a project or just a cheese toastie.

Communicaton is the key to resolving all conflict. Try to think about things from the other person's point of view.

Most people are so busy knocking themselves out trying to do everything they think they should do, they never get around to what they want to do.

Kathleen Winsor

We spend the first twelve months of our children's lives teaching them to walk and talk and the next twelve telling them to sit down and shut up.

Phyllis Diller

The man who doesn't relax and hoot a few hoots voluntarily, now and then, is in great danger of hooting hoots and standing on his head for the edification of the pathologist and trained nurse, a little later on.

Elbert Hubbard

We are so vain that we even care for the opinions of those we don't care for.
Marie Egner von Eschenbach

I like work; it fascinates me. I can sit and look at it for hours.
Jerome K. Jerome

Loafing needs no explanation and is its own excuse.
Christopher Morley

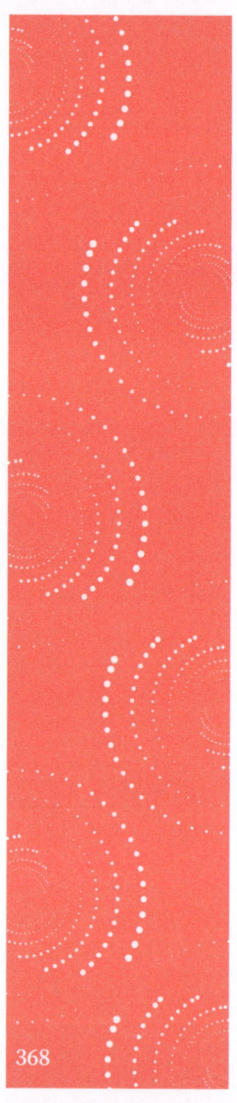

The best cure for insomnia is to get a lot of sleep.
W. C. Fields

It is not enough to be busy.
So are the ants. The question is:
What are we busy about?
Henry David Thoreau

There is a fine line between fishing and just standing on the shore like an idiot.

Steven Wright

When everything seems to be going against you, remember that the airplane takes off against the wind, not with it.

Henry Ford

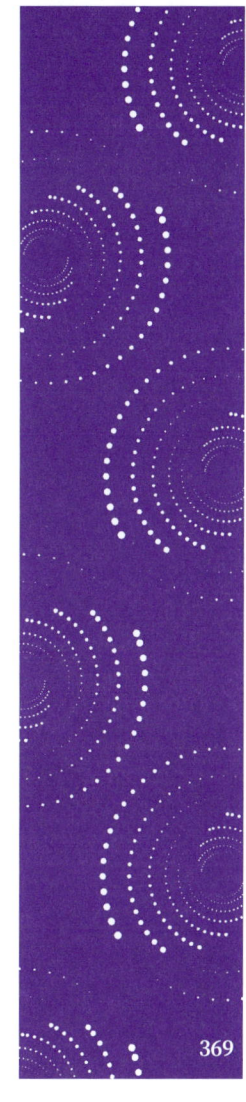

Sometimes you're the windshield; sometimes you're the bug.
Mark Knopfler

Isn't it strange how 'rush hour' is the time when nothing moves?

Make your home into a sanctuary – even if the only calm spot in it is your bathroom.

Sometimes the most important thing in a whole day is the rest we take between two deep breaths.

Etty Hillesum

Cleaning your house while your kids are still growing is like shoveling the walk before it stops snowing.

Phyllis Diller

Smooth seas do not make skilful sailors.
African proverb

There is nothing so annoying as to have two people talking when you're busy interrupting.
Mark Twain

Honk if you hate noise pollution.

The world is full of fools; and he who would not wish to see one, must not only shut himself up alone, but must also break his looking-glass.

Nicolas Boileau

The really idle man gets nowhere. The perpetually busy man does not get much further.

Sir Heneage Ogilvie

There are an enormous number of managers who have retired on the job.
Peter Drucker

How many things are there which I do not want.
Socrates

Try to relax and enjoy the crisis.
Ashleigh Brilliant

I cannot always control what is going on around me but I can always control what I think about what is going on around me.

Lucy MacDonald

Some of the secret joys of living are not found by rushing from point A to point B, but by inventing some imaginary letters along the way.

Douglas Pagels

I go about looking at horses and cattle. They eat grass, make love, work when they have to, bear their young. I am sick with envy of them.

Sherwood Anderson

Don't underestimate the value of Doing Nothing, of just going along, listening to all the things you can't hear, and not bothering.

A. A. Milne

Remember that as a teenager you are in the last stage of your life when you will be happy to hear the phone is for you.
Fran Lebowitz

The British have a remarkable talent for keeping calm, even when there is no crisis.

Franklin P. Jones

Some folks can look so busy doing nothing that they seem indispensable.
Kin Hubbard

If a man insisted always on being serious, and never allowed himself a bit of fun or relaxation, he would go mad or become unstable without knowing it.

Herodotus

The first sign of maturity is the discovery that the volume knob turns down as well as up.

Find a job you like and you add five days to every week.

H. Jackson Brown Jr

The trouble with simple living is that, though it can be joyful, rich, and creative, it isn't simple.

Doris Janzen Longacre

You may not realize it when it happens, but a kick in the teeth may be the best thing in the world for you.

Walt Disney

When I was born I was so surprised I didn't talk for a year and a half.
Gracie Allen

Spring is when you feel like whistling even with a shoe full of slush.
Doug Larson

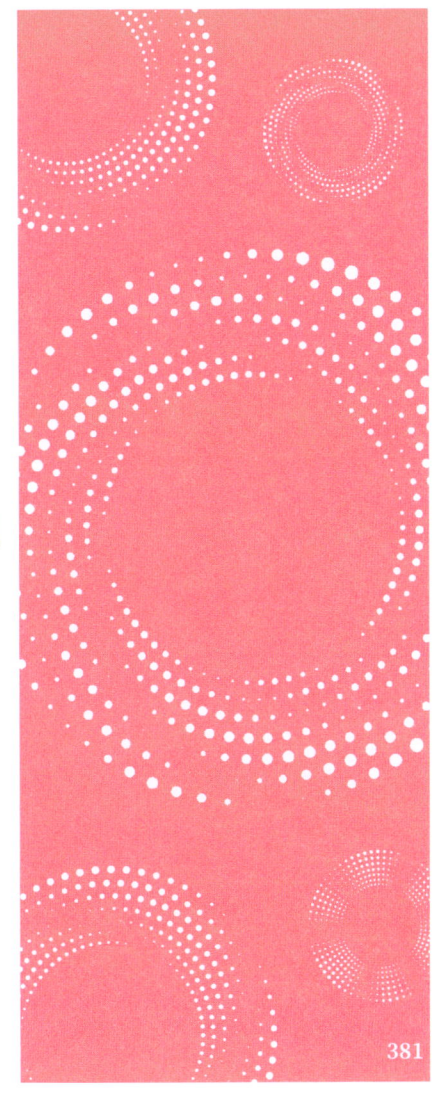

Too often, the opportunity knocks, but by the time you push back the chain, push back the bolt, unhook the two locks and shut off the burglar alarm, it's too late.

Rita Coolidge

The mark of a successful man is one that has spent an entire day on the bank of a river without feeling guilty about it.

While anger can help with a righteous cause, it can also cause internal stress. Pick your battles carefully.

For fast-acting relief, try slowing down.

Lily Tomlin

Reality is frequently inaccurate.

Douglas Adams